THE JUICE
2006

**The Juice
by Matt Skinner**

First published in Great Britain in 2005 by
Mitchell Beazley, an imprint of Octopus Publishing
Group Limited, 2–4 Heron Quays, London E14 4JP.

ISBN: 1 84533 210 5

A CIP catalogue record for this book is available
from the British Library.

The author and publishers will be grateful for any
information which will assist them in keeping future
editions up-to-date. Although all reasonable care
has been taken in the preparation of this book,
neither the publishers nor the author can accept any
liability for any consequences arising from the use
thereof, or the information contained therein.

Photographs by Chris Terry

Commissioning Editor: Hilary Lumsden
Executive Art Editor: Yasia Williams-Leedham
Concept Design: Matt Utber
Layout Design: Tom Green
Index: Hilary Bird
Production: Gary Hayes

Typeset in Swiss 721
Printed and bound by Toppan Printing Company
in China

Contents

Introduction 5

How it all Works 6

The Juice Awards 8

Wine of the Year 9

Producer of the Year 9

Best Value Wine of the Year 10

The Varieties 11

The Whites 11

The Reds 17

The Hot 100 22

Skint top 25 wines for as little money as possible 24

Brownie Points top 25 wines when first impressions mean everything 66

TV Dinners top 25 wines to have with Friday night take-away 106

Bling top 25 wines when money is no object 148

Index 190

Cheers 192

The Juice 2006 – 100 wines you should be drinking

Welcome to *The Juice 2006* – the big kids' survival guide to planet wine. Over the coming pages you won't find any fancy symbols, no intricately detailed maps, and certainly no weird and confusing jargon indicating which lunar cycle to drink your prized bottles in! Sorry.

What you will find is a rundown of the hottest 100 wines (in my opinion) currently gracing the shelves of your local store. Big wines, little wines, fat wines, skinny wines, wines for love, wines for living large, wines for loose change, wines for partying, wines perfect for Tuesday nights in front of the telly… wines you shouldn't just know about… wines you should be drinking.

The Juice began life, and remains, a free weekly email (find it at www.lovewinedrinkbetter.com) that unashamedly celebrates the fact that wine is for everyone, and that awesome wine doesn't have to come with an awesome price tag. And, while great wine is made right around our planet, laying your hands on a few killer bottles shouldn't see you having to scour the earth in order to find them – although I'm sure there are plenty of worse ways you could be spending your weekends. *The Juice* is about how wine fits into your life and not the other way around. It's about trying new things, and most importantly, it's about helping you to drink better.

So, make room for it in your back pocket, your CD rack, your handbag (or man bag!), your car glove box – wherever it will fit! This is *The Juice*, please enjoy, use, and abuse it.'

How it all Works

Rarely would a week go past where someone from our office wouldn't ask me for a wine tip. I was constantly writing down names of wines for colleagues to check out – there had to be an easier way to reach them all! And so, based on what most of my workmates spend on wine, where they buy it from, and how it fits into their lives, *The Juice* – a weekly inter-company email containing three wine recommendations linked by a common theme – was born.

OK, so here's the low down. This guide is a compilation of all the best bits from the weekly *Juice* in 2004 and 2005. To make life simpler, I've broken up the original emails, narrowed the wine recommendations to 100, and then re-jigged them all back into one handy little book for you to take shopping.

We thought that rather than ranking the wines 1–100, it would be far more useful to group the wines by occasion. And so to start with I've split the top 100 wines into four easy groups of twenty-five: Skint, Brownie Points, TV Dinners, and Bling. Let's face it – more often than not it's one of these four (love, food, too little or too much money) that motivates us to buy wine in the first place.

Listed stockists are a mix of supermarkets, national wine chains, and smaller independent wine retailers (the guys who really need your support) – the idea being that you should be able to get your hands on one of the following 100 wines without too much trouble.

Price, vintage, and availability are as accurate as possible at the time of publication. Please also keep updated on this information on my website: www.lovewinedrinkbetter.com.

Happy Drinking!

The Juice Awards

We thought that it was important to hand out a couple of gongs to a few individuals – some of whom in the past year have raised the bar just that extra few notches, and others who simply manage to do it year in year out.

To make it fair, all 100 wines listed in this edition of *The Juice* were tasted "blind" by a hardened team of seasoned professionals in order to determine the awards. Scores were tallied, debates begun, friendships damaged, debates raged on, sleep was lost, and much hair was pulled out in the process. Finally, we were left with two stand-out wines and one stand-out producer in the chosen categories.

Here are the wines that in 2005 rocked our collective worlds.

Enjoy.

WINE OF THE YEAR

Zonte's Footstep Shiraz/Viognier
2003 – South Australia, Australia

Currently Shiraz/Viognier blends are as popular and as common as iPods, and no matter which corner of the earth you venture to, you'll undoubtedly find someone making one somewhere, somehow – I say somehow because during winemaking you have the choice to either blend finished Shiraz with a tiny percentage of finished Viognier or, you head down the traditional Northern Rhône road (as in this case) and ferment the two grapes together. Following the hugely popular 2002 vintage, this wine – put together by Aussie wine duo Zar Brooks and Ben Riggs – pushes all the right buttons at a very keen price. Loaded with inky, ripe raspberry and plum fruit, fresh ground pepper, and apricot aromas – you'll be hard pressed to do better, at even double the money.

PRODUCER OF THE YEAR

Torres – Penedès, Spain

Racking up no less than four entries in this year's edition, when it comes to consistency and value across the board, Spanish wine giant Torres rarely, if ever, misses a beat. From entry-level wonders such as Sangre de Toro, Viña Sol, Atrium Merlot, and Viña Esmeralda right the way through to the Cabernet-based jewel in the company's crown, Mas La Plana, the attention to detail is precise and evident. The recent application of screwcaps for the whites has been a welcome addition and only cements the kind of global attitude that has won the company legions of fans right around the planet. It will come as little surprise that the much-loved Sangre de Toro – the company's biggest seller – is currently celebrating its fiftieth birthday. I've been drinking it for at least ten years and it's never looked better.

BEST VALUE WINE OF THE YEAR

Viña Rodríguez Basa 2004 – Rueda, Spain

Price is a key factor in *The Juice* and so the award for best value is far and away the hardest to win. There were many contenders from right around the planet. Greece, South Africa, Italy, and Australia were all in the final cut, but in the end the wine that has taken this year's *Juice* award in this category is no other than the jaw-droppingly good Viña Rodríguez Basa Blanco 2004 from the Rueda region in Spain. It won for a couple of reasons. While Spain still has much to prove in the white department, this wine delivers the kind of quality that you might expect to find in a Kiwi example for double the money or more. Add to that Rodríguez's rapid and unrelenting pursuit of quality across a range of both regions and price points, and you begin to see why we love this wine.

The Varieties

Just like people, wine comes in all different shapes and sizes. Big wines, little wines, fat wines skinny wines, good wines, great wines – wines that will absolutely blow your mind. And while what happens in the winery plays a big role in determining how a wine might end up tasting, each variety (a bit like people) has its own distinctive personality – personality that you can taste!

With near on 1,000 grapes varieties grown around the planet, here is a brief run down of the most popular along with a few extra that have popped up in this year's *Juice*.

Step outside your comfort zone and try a few new varieties.

Happy Drinking!

THE WHITES

Chardonnay (*shar-don-ay*)

Love it or loathe it, you just can't deny this variety its place in wine's Hall of Fame. The very best examples hail from France's Holy Grail of wine, Burgundy, where texture, finesse, structure, and ageing ability rule rather than simple "drink now" fruit flavours. You see, Chardonnay comes in all different shapes and sizes. Flavours can range from the delicate, citrussy, and slightly honeyed styles of Chablis through to the warmer southern hemisphere styles, where aromas range from peaches and pears through to "full throttle" ripe tropical fruits like banana, pineapple, guava, and mango.

Garganega (*gar-gan-ee-ga*)

Superstar producers are thin on the ground in Italy's Soave (*swar-vay*) region where this variety plays a leading role. Historically, Soave has suffered from a reputation of quantity not quality. But that's all set to change with Soave's new winemaking generation producing some of the greatest (and most consistently high quality) white wines anywhere in Italy. With subtle smells of pear, apple, and honeysuckle, Garganega also benefits from a little extra hang time on the vine.

Gewurztraminer (*ger-vertz-tramina*)
Like an oversized drag queen with too much make up, way too much perfume, super high heels, and very little shame, this variety is the flamboyantly camp member of the white grape family! In reality, Gewurtz is one of the superstar varieties of Alsace in France. Going down as one of the more exotic white grape varieties with the best examples oozing aromas of lychee, rose, orange blossom, cinnamon, ginger, and spice. Typically, they'll be rich and weighty in your mouth (due to low natural acidity) and have great length of flavour.

Grüner Veltliner (*grew-ner velt-lee-ner*)
If you haven't heard of Grüner Veltliner, where have you been?! The uber-cool variety of the moment, its made in Austria and is often likened to Chardonnay for its weight and intensity, but it's spicier with smells of miso paste, ginger, and wet wool.

Marsanne
Clean, fresh, fruity, this grape plays second fiddle to Viognier in France's Northern Rhône Valley, however it dominates many of the white wine blends of the Southern Rhône. Expect ripe peachy fruit flavours, fresh acidity, and barely a whiff of oak. With a bit of age, Marsanne takes on an amazing honeyed character and becomes slightly oilier with more weight and richness. Outside of France, you might see Marsanne pop up in parts of Australia.

Muscat
Muscat can be split into non-identical triplets – Muscat Blanc à

Petit Grains, Muscat of Alexandria, and Muscat Ottonel. Wine styles range from the light and fizzy Mosacto d'Asti of northwest Italy, the sweet and spirity Muscat Beaumes de Venise from France's Rhône Valley, the heady and aromatic Malagas from Spain, the treacle-like Moscatel di Jerez, through to the unique and ancient fortified Muscats of Australia's northeast Victoria.

Pedro Ximenez (pedro him-en-eth)
Although "PX" technically falls into the white grape family, this "sun loving" variety produces sweet, thick, and syrupy wines occasionally referred to as "black sherry"'. Great wines are almost black in colour, viscous, and super sweet with intense aromas of raisin and spice.

Pinot Blanc (pee-no blonk)
As the distant love child of Pinot Gris (which happens to be the brother of Pinot Noir), Pinot Blanc is widely planted in many parts of Europe – especially Alsace in France. PB tends to be pretty neutral in both aroma and flavour. Pears, apples, minerals, honeysuckle – even a slight chalkiness, but what I really love about Pinot Blanc is that it's dangerously easy to drink!

Pinot Gris/Pinot Grigio (pee-no gree/pee-no gree-jee-o)
Technically speaking, these are the same. The key difference comes down to a question of style. Pinot Grigio by definition is light, delicate, and fresh, usually made in stainless-steel tanks and best drunk young while it's really zippy and vibrant. Pinot Gris on the other hand, is fatter and richer with more weight and intensity – often from time spent in oak. Pinot Grigio is commonly found in the cool of Italy's northeast, while Pinot Gris is never more at home than in the French region of Alsace.

Riesling (reez-ling)
Kicking off at the top with the Kenny G of white grapes – technically

brilliant but thought of as pretty daggy. Riesling currently represents some of this planet's great bargain wine buys. While the spiritual home of this variety is Germany, you'll also find world-class examples from Austria, France, and Australia. The best examples will have beautiful, pure, citrus-fruit aromas alongside fresh-cut flowers and spice, while you'll find flavours of lemons, limes, and minerals.

Roussanne (roos-ann)

Rousanne and Marsanne – like their Rhône cousin Viognier – are all about subtle aromatics and textures. Expect a full-bodied white choc full of stone fruits (think apricots, peaches) and spice. Some examples will come with a decent dose of alcohol, due to late ripening.

Sauvignon Blanc (sov-in-yon blonk)

Passion-fruit, gooseberry, elderflower, blackcurrant, sweaty armpits, even cat's pee (really!). France, South Africa, Chile, Australia all have a good crack, but New Zealand – Marlborough to be exact – is the undeniable new home of this variety where the best examples are pale in colour and unmistakably pungent on the nose. Typically these wines are painfully crisp, clean, and ultra refreshing with plenty of zip and racy acidity.

Sémillon (semi-on)

Sémillon is native to France's Bordeaux region, but it's down under in New South Wales' Hunter Valley district where Semillon (no é this time) has had greatest success, producing beautifully crafted and insanely long-lived wines. In its youth, great examples explode with pear, white peach, and other ripe summer fruits. But stash a couple of bottles away for that rainy day in a few years time, and that's when you'll witness its true magic – aromas of super-intense citrus fruit, even marmalade, alongside toast, honey, nuts, and sweet spice.

Verdicchio (*ver-dik-ee-o*)

Verdicchio is grown and produced in Italy's Marche region – big rich whites that are pretty neutral when it comes to aroma, but super lemony in flavour with spice and richness. Because of its weight, it can handle oak too, so expect to see some wooded examples.

Viognier (*vee-on-yeah*)

Viognier overflows with intoxicating aromas of apricots, orange rind, and fresh-cut flowers. It's weighty, rich, and oily in your mouth, with great length of flavour and beautiful soft acidity. Native to France's Northern Rhône, it also shows lots of promise in Australia and South Africa.

THE REDS

Barbera (*bar-bear-a*)

Barbera is bright and cherryish in both aroma and taste, while nearly always carrying trademark super-fresh acidity and lowish tannins. Far from being exclusive to Italy's northwest, Barbera grows throughout the country and other continents, with Australia's King Valley being home to some of the oldest Barbera vines to be found outside of Italy.

Cabernet Sauvignon (*kab-er-nay sov-in-yon*)

Cabernet is ruler of the red grapes – the best display power, finesse, elegance, the ability to age, and universal appeal. Its real home is in France's Bordeaux, but particularly good examples also come from Italy, Spain, Chile, Argentina, South Africa, Australia, and California. The range of flavours and aromas varies greatly, however look for blackcurrant, dark cherry, and plumy fruit alongside cedar, mint, and eucalyptus.

Carmènere (car-man-yeah)

Carmènere can be a complete nightmare in the vineyard – it's hard to get ripe, and once it is you have a tiny window in which to pick it before the acidity disappears. But when it's good, it's really good! Bearing an uncanny likeness to Merlot, the best examples are bursting with super-dark fruits (think plums, blackberries, and dark cherries) together with aromas of spice and leather.

Grenache (gren-ash)

Grenache has been around for donkey's years! Grown widely in Spain, France, and Australia, it's the great workhorse of the red grapes, and a stand-alone performer in its own right. Making concentrated, weighty, fully-fledged reds, especially in France's Southern Rhône the wines sit comfortably alongside some of the greatest in the world. The "big G" also makes many rosés, where tannin, a bit of colour, zippy acidity – even a good whack of alcohol – are perfect for pink wines.

Malbec (mal-bec)

This is a variety that loves the sun and is found in Argentina's Andes mountains (home to a handful of the highest altitude vineyards planted anywhere). These are big wines, and the best examples are soft and super fruity with plums and spice.

Merlot (mer-low)

For many years Merlot has very much played second fiddle to big brother Cabernet, often sidelined for blending. Merlot is the most widely planted red grape in Bordeaux, and in recent times, both California and Australia have developed a love affair with it. New World examples tend to be plump with ripe, plummy fruit and naturally low tannins. Wines hailing from north of the equator will be drier, leaner, and less in your face.

Mourvèdre (more-ved-ra)

This is the superstar of France's Southern Rhône. Together with dark, sweet fruit there's mushroom, tobacco, Mum's lamb roast, and even the elephant enclosure at the zoo! In Spain it's known as Monastrell and Mataro, while in Australia it goes by the names Mataro and Mourvèdre. Because of its funkiness it's rarely produced as a solo variety and is usually reserved for blending.

Nebbiolo (*neb-ee-olo*)
The best examples are layered and complex, oozing aromas of tar, roses, dark cherry, black olives, and rosemary – basically, they smell incredible! In great wines, a combination of concentrated fruit, firm acidity, and a wash of drying tannins will ensure they go the distance if you want to stash them away. Nebbiolo's home is Piedmont (food heaven) where it's great with a broad range of food styles from mushrooms (Piedmont is home to the truffle) to chicken, rabbit, and all sorts of game right through to old and mouldy cheeses.

Negroamaro (*neg-ro-maro*)
Alongside Nero d'Avola and Primitivo, Negroamaro (black bitter) is winning "I'd like my mine with balls please" fans the world over! The best examples of Negroamaro tend to come turbo charged with smells of tar, morello cherry, and Mediterranean spice and earth. So far Sicily is having all the fun with this variety.

Pinot Meunier (*pee-no moon-yeah*)
Another blending variety, this is the magical third party in Champagne, completing the triangle with Chardonnay and Pinot Noir. In small doses it adds a rich nuttiness that gives weight and intensity. Outside of France there are only a handful of places, such as Australia, Germany, and New Zealand where its grown.

Pinot Noir (*pee-no nwar*)
Great examples of Pinot are seductive, intriguing – even sexy – and their versatility with food is

nearly unrivalled. Considered to be one of the lightest red varieties, the best show layer upon layer of strawberry, raspberry, plum, and dark forest fruits, with aromas of earth, spice, animal, cedar, and truffle. These wines range from delicate and minerally through to silky and rich, Check out examples from France's Côte de Nuits (Burgundy), Australia's Tasmania and NZ's Central Otago and Martinborough regions.

Primitivo/Zinfandel (*prima-tee-vo*)

For a long time we just kind of assumed that these two kids were in fact distinctly different varieties, although findings from recent research has shown that these grapes are in fact twins! Zinfandel (Zin for short) is found in the mighty US of A, where most things big are seen as beautiful! In Italy's south Primitivo holds its head high alongside fellow red varieties Negroamaro and Nero d'Avola. With plenty of sweet, ripe fruit and

aromas of violets and leather, this style is much more restrained than its transatlantic brother.

Sangiovese (*san-gee-o-vay-zee*)

Characteristically loaded with aromas of dark cherry, plum, and forest fruits Sangiovese often also smells of tobacco, spice, and earth. Most people remember Sangiovese for its trademark "super-drying" tannins, which, without the help of food, can make this variety a hard old slog. It's native to Tuscany, where it shines as Chianti Classico and Brunello di Monatlcino. More recently, it has also surfaced in Australia and the USA, however so far it hasn't quite had the success abroad that it enjoys at home.

Syrah/Shiraz (*si-rar/sher-az*)

Technically the same, Syrah is the French name for this variety. Typically Syrah is lighter in body, and aromas include redcurrants, raspberry, and plum, and nearly always super-dooper white pepper and spice. Shiraz tends to be concentrated and ripe, intense in colour and at its best oozes aromas of blood plum, raspberry, earth, cedar, and freshly ground pepper. Some New World wine makers are now also calling their wines Syrah, to reflect the difference in style from Shiraz.

Tempranillo (*tem-pra-nee-o*)

Tempranillo is the grand-old man of the Spanish wine scene. Native to Spain's Rioja region it's also sunk its roots in nearby Ribera del Duerro, Navarra, and Priorat. Typically, it has a solid core of dark berried fruits complete with a rustic edge that relies on savoury aromas such as tobacco, spice, leather, and earth. Recently the trend has been to make international styles with big colour, big fruit, big oak – big everything!

The Hot 100

Skint

Brownie Points

TV Dinners

Bling

Wines for as little money as possible

Yes there's still such a thing as good value – plenty of it in fact, you just have to know where to look. You might be hard up, pay day might still be some weeks off, never ending bills might have left you dry, or maybe you just can't stomach spending any more than you have to on a bottle of wine. Whatever the reason, this chapter should turn what could be a nightmarish game of "Skint Supermarket Russian Roulette" into something far more rewarding.

Torres
Viña Esmeralda 2003
Penedès
Spain

get it from…

United Kingdom
£5.50

Tesco

PRODUCER OF THE YEAR

A virtual essay in smells of jasmine, rose, musk, and orange, this wine is an exotic mix of white varieties Muscadet and Gewurztraminer (try saying that after a couple of bottles!).

Year in, year out, this wine effortlessly delivers consistency while drawing a great big line in the sand between it and the ocean of wishy washy whites at the same price point.

Bone dry and really refreshing, Viña Esmerelda is best drunk nice and chilled – but remember not too cold or you'll mask all those amazing aromatics mentioned above.

Casillero del Diablo
Cabernet Sauvignon 2003
Maipo
Chile

get it from…

United Kingdom
£5.49

Oddbins

The story goes that the founder of
Torres wines, Don Melchor spread
a rumour amongst his workers that
the Devil himself lived in Melchor's
private wine cellar. Unlikely, but
funnily enough Melchor never had
much wine go missing after that.
Clever!

Paying homage to Melchor's so-
called tenant, this wine – made in
mega quantities – is one of Concha
y Toro's biggest sellers.

On board you'll fine plenty of dark
plum and cassis-like fruit alongside
a decent slug of good charry oak –
great, old-fashioned everyday red
at its best.

Dr Loosen
"L" Riesling 2003
Mosel
Germany

It's time to leave any pre-conceived ideas you might have had about German wine out the window, because Germany is (and always has been) home to some of the slickest Riesling producers on the planet.

In the "good value" camp this wine – hammered together by Ernie Loosen (the Riesling world's answer to Obi-Wan Kenobi!) – is a stunner.

"Dr L" is squeaky clean, a little bit limey, and just the faintest bit sweet, all of which help to catapult this wine into "Sunday morning dim sum superstar" territory.

La Guita
Manzanilla NV
Sanlúcar de Barrameda
Spain

get it from…

United Kingdom
£3.99 (37.5cl)

Bermann Wine Cellars

As one of the most popular styles of sherry on the market, the best examples of manzanilla – like fino – are bone dry, nutty, slightly salty, and really awesome with foods like olives, anchovies, capers, cured meats, and nuts.

Both manzanilla and fino are best drunk young and fresh (ask your retailer) and should always be served nice and cold.

Smaller bottles are better than big ones to aid freshness, and a screwcap – which many examples now sport – is another massive plus for all the same reasons.

La Baume
Viognier 2004
Languedoc
France

Way down in France's southwest, local co-operative La Baume crank out some pretty handy wines at some even handier prices.

This wine is everything you might expect from a far more expensive southern hemisphere example – clean, well made, and complete with trademark Viognier vivaciousness.

White peach, apricot, and orange are what you can expect to smell, while in your mouth it's clean – not cloying like some – and dry. Best of all is the ultra sexy price tag!

get it from…

United Kingdom
£5.50

Tesco

Torres
Sangre de Toro 2003
Penedès
Spain

PRODUCER OF THE YEAR

Currently celebrating its fiftieth anniversary, legendary Spanish red Sangre de Toro (blood of the bull), would, without question, go down as one of the all time great bargain wine buys.

A chunky mix of Spanish grapes Garnacha and Cariñena (and without the addition of blood!), this wine is loaded with aromas of raspberry, plum, pepper, and spice.

Take a sip to see a not too heavy mouthful of sweet lush fruit that wraps itself up in a clean, dry, happy ending. Happy fiftieth Sangre!

get it from…

United Kingdom
£5.69

Tesco

**Brown Brothers
Moscato 2004
Victoria
Australia**

Think fresh, sweet grape juice, add a few little bubbles, and there you have it in simple terms – Moscato!

As a member of the great big Muscat clan, Moscato is not as sweet as some desert wines and no where near as fizzy as Champagne – anything but highbrow, Moscato, for exactly that reason, is one of my all time fave wines.

As a native to Piedmont in northwestern Italy, the best thing about this grape is the feather-light 5 degrees of alcohol that most examples of Moscato sport – a third of what many wines carry… some of my mates would say that just means you can drink three times as much!

Umani Ronchi Verdicchio dei
Castelli di Jesi
Casal di Serra 2003
Umbria
Italy

get it from…
United Kingdom
£4.99

Sainsbury's

Italy may well have forged its reputation off the back of a dizzying range of great reds, but lovers of clean, dry, racy whites should head straight for the nearest booze aisle to check out this unbelievably good-value white that lifts the lid on just how good parts of this country can be in the white department.

Lemonish to look at, the nose is fresh and floral with plenty of ripe peach and citrus fruit. In the mouth it's rich, dry, and super versatile with a broad range of food styles.

Dangerously good!

Chivite Gran Feudo
Rosé 2004
Navarra
Spain

get it from…

United Kingdom
£5.50

Oddbins

I love rosé. I love it because
generally it's pretty cheap. I love it
because it's great with a whole
range of ingredients. But most of all
I love rosé because at a certain time
of the year increased sightings of
pink wine consumption pretty much
signal that summer's either here
or just around the corner!

And if you still find yourself in need
of convincing, you'll impress the
pants off anyone (easy tiger) with
your "up-to-the-minute" knowledge
of wine fashion.

Rosé rocks! Spread the word.

Annie's Lane
Riesling 2004
South Australia
Australia

get it from…

United Kingdom
£7.50

Oddbins

Showing all the hallmarks of great Riesling – lemon, lime, mineral, spice, and a steely-like structure, this wine from South Australia's Clare Valley is a massive winner in anyone's language.

Made by Aussie Riesling dynamo Wendy Stucky, the ultra-friendly Annie's Lane range consistently rates as some of my favourite everyday wines.

Just for the record, these are wines that will hold together beautifully for years to come should you be able to keep your mitts off them!

Merlot Misunderstood
April 25 2005, 12.02pm

From the movie *Sideways*:

Jack: *If they want to drink Merlot, we're drinking Merlot.*

Miles: *No way! If anyone orders Merlot, I'm leaving. I am NOT drinking any fucking Merlot!*

Having recently snatched the crown from Chardonnay as the planet's "love-to-hate" variety of choice, this week *The Juice* asks why Merlot? Apart from helping you get into wine, what did it ever do to you?

Merlot – often planted as a "blender" to soften and round out the much drier Cabernet Sauvignon – skyrocketed into the hearts and mouths of consumers during the 1990s after Californian winemakers had ear-marked it for solo success. Success followed quickly too. Apart from being super easy to say in even the strongest of American accents (*Merrrrr-lowww*), punters loved that actually drinking the stuff was even easier!

Words like soft, juicy, plumy, round, full of fruit, delicious, even gluggable all conspire in "Pied Piper-like" fashion to sweep you up and suck you in. Anything that sounds that good, has to be tried. For the wine novice Merlot is both easy and safe.

But, as we all know, a little bit of knowledge can be a dangerous thing, and, just as with Chardonnay, Merlot has now truly become a victim of its own success. As a result it's reported that sales of Merlot – still the most widely consumed red grape in the USA – are on the slide. And although *Sideways* hasn't helped, a growing wave of public disapproval has been the real killer.

get it from…

United Kingdom
£5.99 (50cl)

Waitrose
widely available

Brown Brothers
Orange Muscat & Flora 2002
Victoria
Australia

Here's one for those of you with a sweet tooth. Jam-packed with aromas of orange rind, apricot, not to mention a whole cupboard full of exotic spices – like a Michael Jackson moonwalk, this wine just kind of slides on through your mouth with seamless ease.

Surely this is one of the best-value sweet wines on the market.

Geoff Merrill
Grenache Rosé 2004
South Australia
Australia

get it from…
United Kingdom
£5.99

Oddbins

Geoff Merrill is a great Australian
with an enormous moustache.
More importantly, he also happens
to be a very good winemaker and
his 2004 vintage is testament to that.

Sealed with a screwcap, this wine
is fresh as a daisy with aromas
and flavours of raspberry and
redcurrants. Then to finish there's
a trademark racy acidity and just
the faintest smack of tannin.

And it's pink – what more could you
ask for! Drink it while the sun shines.

Ravenswood Vintners Blend
Zinfandel 2002
California
USA

get it from…

United Kingdom
£7.49

Waitrose

And for those of you who like your reds bigger than a Hollywood blockbuster, this wine is nothing short of Oscar winning stuff.

Like the great Muhammad Ali, it starts by teasing you with subtle smells of sweet plums and leather before delivering a knockout mouthful of inky dark fruit, liquorice-like intensity, and well-balanced, dry grippy tannins.

In true Ravenswood fashion (their logo being "no wimpy wines"), this is not for the faint of heart!

get it from…

United Kingdom
£4.49

Sainsbury's
widely available

Lindemans Bin 65
Chardonnay 2004
South Australia
Australia

With something like a gazillion or so cases of this great Aussie workhorse pumped out annually, I'm always blown away by how consistently good both the quality and price remain.

As for what it smells and tastes like – think tropical fruit with just the faintest hint of cedary oak – while in your mouth it's ripe and lush with soft acidity and a long dry finish.

I regularly taste Chardonnays ten times the price of this wine that aren't anywhere near as good. Say no more.

Fairview
Goats do Roam 2003
Paarl
South Africa

get it from…
United Kingdom
£4.99

Tesco

Legendary South African winemaker Charles Back's tongue is jammed right against the side of his cheek with this Rhône-style copycat. You see the irony is that goats really do roam on this meticulous Paarl estate – unfortunately his clever sense of humour isn't appreciated by Côte de Rhône traditionalists (they even tried to take action against him!).

Overflowing with bright raspberry-cherry fruit and spice, this is a deliciously drinkable blend of Syrah, Mourvèdre, and the not so Rhône-like Pinotage.

Surely Back's revenge is in knowing just how good this wine really is…

Viña Rodríguez
Basa 2004
Rueda
Spain

BEST VALUE WINE OF THE YEAR

This wine almost reaches out of the glass, grabs you by the throat and says "Damn I'm good!" Well that might be a slight exaggeration, but this wine is simply mind-blowing.

A blend of Sauvignon Blanc and the native Rueda variety Viura, this wine explodes in your face with aromas of passion-fruit, gooseberry, and elderflower. Take a sip and you'll see a lean, tight, ultra-fresh white that's set to become your new favourite white of the summer!

Tatachilla Growers
Semillon/Sauvignon Blanc/
Chenin Blanc 2004
South Australia
Australia

get it from…

United Kingdom
£4.99

Waitrose

This combination of varieties
(Semillon and Sauvignon Blanc)
can at times be about as exciting
as watching paint dry, but the
crew at Tatachilla have risen
to the challenge admirably.

Apples, pears, and those fizzy
lemon sherbet sweets are what
you will smell while in the mouth
it's clean, fresh, dry, and incredibly
well-balanced.

Such a great drink for the money.

St Hallet
Gamekeeper's Red 2003
South Australia
Australia

get it from…

United Kingdom
£5.99

Waitrose

The man behind the controls at St Hallet is Brit ex-pat Matt Gannon, who was last year named young Australian Winemaker of The Year. No mean feat.

And even at the cheap end of his range, Gannon's Midas touch is evident with his first release of the consistently good Gamekeeper's red. As a soft, fruity blend of Grenache, Mataro, Shiraz, and Touriga this is sensational winter party gear that will keep raising eyebrows all night long!

Feels Like Home
August 20 2004, 12.06pm

It's been a big couple of weeks on the road, kicking off in France and winding up in sunny South America. There I was, the sky was blue, the eucalyptus trees smelt really good, people were smiling, kids were surfing, and the sun was beaming down. God it felt good to be home. And over in the distance were The Andes mountains. Hang on. Rewind. The Andes mountains? They're not in Australia…

No they're not, but then again, neither was I. This was South America, Chile in fact.

In case you haven't noticed the growing number of Chilean wines gracing the shelves of your local store, Chile is a wine country on the up big time! Occupying the direct opposite geographical position to Australia in the southern hemisphere, this needle-like strip of land was long producing wine before Australia was even a twitch in his old man's shorts.

But the real advances in Chile's wine scene have only come in the past twenty years since the country emerged from communist rule and began trading freely with the rest of the world. Modern technology was embraced, international winemakers imported, and a global understanding and acceptance of what was going on in places like Australia and the USA was quickly digested.

The new-look Chile has quickly forged a reputation as a dependable producer of good value wines – red and white. And, while international investment from the likes of France and the USA increases, more and more "well-travelled" Chilean winemakers are taking the reins of the country's top estates. Likewise, better-suited varieties and improved viticulture are also helping. All in all, Chile looks in pretty good shape.

get it from…

United Kingdom
£6.99

Liberty Wines
Valvona & Crolla

Cerro del Masso
Chianti 2003
Tuscany
Italy

Alberto Antonini is the man behind many of Italy's most exciting new wines. Unlike a lot of big-name consultant winemakers, Antonini seems to be trying to preserve regional character and finesse rather than creating formulaic wines that – who knows where they're from – might purely exist for points.

This is soft, easy-drinking Sangiovese produced from the Chianti region at large. Alongside aromas of dark cherry and leather you'll find fresh tobacco and spice, and great fruit is underlined by dry, grippy Sangiovese tannins. A new Friday night pizza classic.

Catena
Malbec 2002
Mendoza
Chile

get it from…

United Kingdom
£5.99

Majestic
Bibendum

For those of you who like your reds with a double helping of flavour, check this insanely priced blockbuster from the foothills (at 3,000 ft/915 m!) of the Andes – on the Argentinian side.

Rarely elsewhere does Malbec hit the dizzying highs (sorry, no pun intended) of quality it does in Argentina. A rich and explosive core of soft, sweet dark-berried fruit is the key to success both on the nose and in the mouth.

But wait there's more! Wine from this part of the world is also rumoured to contain the highest level of antioxidants – great for your immune system and perfect for fighting off a whole range of nasties!

United Kingdom
£7.49

Oddbins

Torres Atrium
Merlot 2003
Penedès
Spain

PRODUCER OF THE YEAR

This wine represents all that is good about value-for-money modern Spanish wine, and even Merlot for that matter!

Clearly with an international audience in mind, Atrium is a soft, velvety, and very user-friendly Merlot at a ridiculously user-friendly price. Think sweet plum, blueberry, and spice – and there you have it.

Surely one of the planet's most underrated red wine bargains.

The Whitehorse Inn
February 25 2005, 12.50pm

Bit of a sad one this week Juicers, with news that The Whitehorse Inn – home of my first ever job in wine – is set to close its doors forever.

Now if you're in the northern hemisphere, you should probably know that this pub makes the London East End "local" look a bit like The Ritz. Saturday nights at "The Horse" were legendary. Home to one of the worst local footy clubs, the struggling Horse became a haven for underagers and a continual string of deadbeat ex-crims.

From the legendary "Skinner-poured" Southern Comfort and lemonades (5 parts Southern: 1 part lemonade) to one of the biggest "all-in brawls" I've ever seen, closing time at The Horse simply meant me having to sweep up a sea of broken pool cues, blood, glass, and hair! But it was the little things about The Horse that made it great. Most of the locals were too lazy to walk to the toilets, and so instead would just go in the ashtrays provided by the bar.

One of the guys in the blues band (Saturday nights) used to sell most of the customers and staff drugs, and then there was Chuck, one of the barmen, who told me that if I ever needed a car then he "had a couple of mates down the docks that could sort me some wheels for a few hundred bucks…"

But, colourful stuff aside, it was because of the manager who told me that I needed to "get tasting" and the Mark Shield wine guides I used to read to pass time in the bottle shop that I'll never forget The Whitehorse Inn.

get it from…

United Kingdom
£5.99

Waitrose

The Naked Grape
Riesling 2004
Pfalz
Germany

Another value-packed example from German superstar, Ernie Loosen (remember Obi-Wan, p.29!).

This time round, the magic unfolds in the form of a super-light and mouth-watering, mineral-tipped Riesling from the Pfalz – a German region renowned for producing slightly richer wines than the nearby Mosel.

The faintest hint of sweetness means that alongside food styles that employ all those ultra-fresh and aromatic ingredients like lime, coriander, ginger, lemongrass, and chilli, you will struggle to go better.

Porcupine Ridge
Syrah 2004
Franschhoek
South Africa

get it from…

United Kingdom
£6.99

Waitrose
Oddbins

Highly drinkable blends of Syrah/
Shiraz (and most without the
influence of oak) in all shapes
and sizes are charming the pants
off punters right around the world
at the moment.

Complete with super-dooper
raspberry and black pepper
character, this bargain-priced wine
from the stables of South African
guns Boekenhoutskloof is more
than worthy of your attention.

Montana
Sauvignon Blanc 2004
Marlborough
New Zealand

get it from…

United Kingdom
£6.99

Oddbins

New Zealand is the home of
Sauvignon Blanc's new breed
of hero, but finding affordable
examples can be a pretty tricky task.

Enter NZ wine-giant Montana. And
what's really refreshing to see is that
big company influence hasn't come
at the expense of the wine. Sporting
all the hallmarks of great Sauvignon
Blanc: passion-fruit, gooseberry,
elderflower, and fresh herbs, this
wine has the added bonus of
being insanely affordable.

The nifty screwcap ensures the wine
is as fresh as the winemaker
intended you to see it.

Grab some while you can.

get it from…

United Kingdom
£6.99

Waitrose
Majestic

Yalumba Viognier 2003
South Australia
Australia

Viognier – a variety native to France's Northern Rhône Valley – has recently shown heaps of promise in a few Aussie vineyards.

Yalumba is perhaps Australia's finest producer of this variety, and right across a range of price points. Its base range – from which this wine comes – is, in a word, sensational.

Displaying intense aromas of apricot, orange rind, and fresh-cut flowers, the palate is typically oily and rich with great length of flavour balanced beautifully by soft natural acidity. A cracker.

Riesling – The Comeback Kid
April 4 2004, 1.15pm

Even though I buy wine for a living, when it comes to choosing wine to take to a friend's place, there are few jobs that freak me out more. I'm not really sure why? Perhaps it's a bit of that "under the microscope" feeling (sorry friends!) or maybe it's just a case of not wanting to disappoint, but for whatever the reason it's a difficult task that always seems to take me ages! Just ask Carls…

Recently when I've been in this situation, I'll find myself diving into the fridge of my local store and coming out armed with a bottle of Riesling. Yep, Riesling!

For many years Riesling has kind of been like the "Kenny G" of white grape varieties – technically brilliant, but a whole lot daggy. Add to this a couple of good old-fashioned wine scandals in the 1970s – not forgetting that most people remember this variety as being "sweet" – and many punters will give Riesling the biggest-of-big thumbs down.

However, for more than just a few years now Riesling has been on the comeback, and apart from being awesome value for money, as a food friendly variety – especially with a handful of Asian flavours – you'll struggle to do better.

Brownie Points

When first impressions mean everything!

You've got a new girlfriend, a pay rise is on the cards, you're meeting the "in-laws-to-be" for the very first time, you're off to dinner with friends who know a bit about wine, you need to make an apology, a bribe… Perhaps it's for love, maybe it's for money, it might even be for both – whatever the reason, the following twenty-five wines are for when first impressions mean absolutely everything.

Guigal
Côtes du Rhône 2000
Rhône
France

get it from…

United Kingdom
£7.99

Booths
Oddbins

Fresh from the stables of Marcel Guigal's space-age winery in the Northern Rhône, this has to be without doubt one of France's – if not the world's – most consistently good red wine buys.

Varieties Grenache, Syrah, and Mourvèdre combine to work here with all the style, skill, and synchronization you'd expect from the Beastie Boys.

Jam-packed with aromas and flavours of raspberry, dark cherry, and freshly ground black pepper, it's hard to believe the rumour that they pump out in excess of 500,000 cases of this wine annually, without compromising quality.

Go you good thing!

get it from…

United Kingdom
£8.59

Oddbins

Kostas Lazaridis
Amethystos Dry White 2000
Macedonia
Greece

The Greek wine scene has never looked in better shape. Improved work in the vineyards, new winemaking equipment, and a global perspective have resulted in the production of a handful of world-class wines.

And this example is no exception. Slung together from a mix of Sémillon, Sauvignon Blanc, and native variety Assyrtiko – think light, fresh, and dry, with a great intensity of ripe-apple and pear-like fruit.

If the sun's shining in your part of the world, be sure to grab some!

Wirra Wirra
Church Block Cabernet
Sauvignon/Shiraz/Merlot 2002
South Australia
Australia

get it from…

United Kingdom
£8.99

Sainsbury's

With a wine like this, it's really no surprise that Wirra winemaker Samantha Connew was a finalist in the 2004 "Qantas Australian Winemaker of the Year" award.

Made from a blend of Cabernet Sauvignon, Shiraz, and Merlot this wine is mid-weight and bursting at the seams with aromas and flavours of sweet plum, raspberry, chocolate, and spice. You'd be hard pressed to do better for the money. The fact that the wine also wears a screwcap just makes it even better!

The Rodney Dangerfield and Dugald MacKenzie edition

If you've ever been lucky enough to have me bombard you with lines from *Caddyshack*, then you'll probably realize that it's a bit of a sad day with news last week that comic genius, Rodney Dangerfield passed away aged eighty-two.

Undoubtedly, Dangerfield's true golden moment came as construction magnate, Al Cervic in the modern cinematic masterpiece, *Caddyshack*. Now, those of you who are thinking "Skinner must be on drugs if he thinks Caddyshack falls into the modern cinematic masterpiece category" should probably re-consider that thought. I happen to know plenty of *Juice* readers who feel much the same way as I do about this film – in fact if you don't remember this movie as being particularly funny, then I suggest you go and hire it out this weekend and give it another shot.

Just take the following Dangerfield *Caddyshack* quotes for example: "Ah, this is the worst lookin' hat I ever saw! I bet you buy a hat like this you get a free bowl of soup, huh? Oh it looks good on you, though." "Tell the cook this is low-grade dog food – this steak still has marks were the jockey was hittin' it." "Oh, this your wife… you musta been something before electricity." "This your grandson… now I know why tigers eat their young."

Yes I'm easily amused, but I'm crying with laughter again for only about the ten millionth time, and with lines like the above how could you not be! If you're finding all of this a case of "I guess you just had to be there", then follow the link to www.carlspackler.com – my favourite *Caddyshack* website – and head for the multimedia section.

get it from…

United Kingdom
£6.80

Sainsbury's

Stella Bella
Semillon/Sauvignon Blanc 2003
Western Australia
Australia

Margaret River superstar Janice McDonald really delivers the goods here with the super-value, high-quality Stella Bella range.

Passion-fruit, pear, and peach combine to star in this fresh, dry white that provides a brilliant springboard for a whole range of amazing foodstuffs from the sea.

And with the Sauvignon Blanc component of the blend having spent a little time in wood, this wine achieves an extra dimension of flavour that many others twice the price don't.

Veramonte Primus
Carmenère/Cabernet Sauvignon/
Merlot 2002
Casablanca
Chile

Chile has a lot going for it: great climate, unlimited water supply, a great big ocean running the entire length of its western side, and an incredible mix of grape varieties – traditional, and not so traditional.

Chilean winemakers have mixed opinions about local red variety Carmenère (*car-man-yeah*), but nearly all agree that when it's made really well, it's awesome! Thankfully for us, this wine falls head first into the "awesome" camp. Lush, fruity, and loaded with aromas of dark-currants, sweet-cherry, tobacco, and leather.

If you're a fan of Merlot, and fancy trying a new but similar variety, this one is definitely worth a look.

Giesen
Sauvignon Blanc 2004
Canterbury
New Zealand

get it from…

United Kingdom
£6.64

Tesco

Fuelling the current global love
for New Zealand Sauvignon Blanc,
this insanely priced New World
white ticks all the right boxes.

Clean, crisp, dry, and screwcaped –
translating into wine so fresh it hurts.

And as added bonus, if you ever
happen to find yourself lost or
looking for sheep in Canterbury
(probably just my Kiwi mate
Campbell), then you'll be glad
of the local map that doubles
as the front label!

Vasse Felix
Cabernet/Merlot 2001
Western Australia
Australia

Just like the pounding swell that batters the Margaret River peninsula in Western Australia, this wine is a truly consistent performer, and spot-on for any of you who fancy your reds carrying a few extra kilos.

Big colour (purple/black) and big aroma (full-throttle cassis and cedar) give way to a mouthful of sweet dark-berryish fruit that hangs inside longer than Sunny Garcia at Pipeline, before rolling out into a balanced drying finish.

Any ride that good gets a perfect ten, Vasse Felix!

Zonte's Footstep
Shiraz/Viognier 2003
South Australia
Australia

get it from...
United Kingdom
£7.59

Sainsbury's

WINE OF THE YEAR

Shiraz (red grape)/Viognier (white grape) blends are popping up with all the frequency of reality TV programmes. Some are good, many are terrible.

One of the hottest newcomers to the Oz wine scene is Zonte's Footstep. The addition of a shiny, bright-red screwcap has only helped preserve it's super-dooper raspberry, apricot, and black pepper character.

A couple of glasses and you'll know exactly why this wine sports a trophy cupboard that could rival even the likes of the Aussie cricket team!

The Italian Job
April 29 2005, 12.23pm

Tickets for this year's Glastonbury sold out in just three hours, during which time festival-lovers around the UK pounded their redial buttons harder than Campbell might pound his liver on a typical Tuesday evening.

It's festival time for the wine industry too, and the week before last saw Verona play host to Planet Earth's largest wine trade show – the Grand Daddy of wine expos, Vinitaly!

For five days 4,000 producers squeeze into ten huge warehouses pouring endless samples of Italy's latest offerings to a 250,000-strong army of wine buyers from around the world. And while Glastonbury it's not you'll have to flip a coin as to which one is more taxing on your body. It's a grueling schedule that swallows up and spits out even some of the hardest professionals!

A typical Vinitaly day might see you drag yourself out of bed as close to the 8am (leaving deadlines as tight as possible), enjoy a nutritious breakfast of espresso coffee, have multiple near-death experiences in the Verona morning traffic, queue and order (in your worst Italian and much to everyone's amusement) coffee for everybody but yourself – only realizing once you've dealt them out, taste and write notes on a lazy eighty or so wines or until your teeth start to ache and/or you fall asleep, go out to dinner and enjoy yet another simple thirteen-course *degustation* menu, use the car trip home (the one you'd had marked for sleep) for singing your heart and lungs out to the "saccharin sounds" of The Eagles, and finally stop at the hotel bar on the way to your room for "just one quick drink" before eventually being ordered to bed at 3.30am by the hotel's night porter.

It's very easy to become your own worst enemy! Or so I've heard…

Bonny Doon
Big House Red 2002
Santa Cruz
USA

get it from…

United Kingdom
£8.55

Selfridges
Philglass & Swiggot
Berry Bros & Rudd

The world really does need more Randall Grahm's. As one of my all-time wine heroes – mainly for his refreshingly welcome (and often eccentric) take on the wine world – Grahm effortlessly knits together serious winemaking with Monty Python-like attitude.

Influenced little by what goes on in his own backyard, yet driven by what happens throughout Europe, this wine is a soft, super-fruity, screwcapped mix of about a dozen different red varieties.

get it from…

United Kingdom
£8.79

Oddbins

Metala
Shiraz/Cabernet 2002
South Australia
Australia

Lesson – vines are a bit like people. While young vines are full of energy, older vines aren't and lose their ability to produce large volumes of grapes. What old vines do produce though often ends up being heavily concentrated.

This wine hails from Langhorne Creek in South Australia where 100-plus year-old vines create some very serious wines. Blacker than the late great Johnny Cash, this wine is of gigantic proportions. A super solid core of liquorice, cassis, smoke, and prune, give way to mouthful of wine that that you just about need a knife and fork for!

get it from…

United Kingdom
£8.99

Philglass & Swiggot

Mudhouse
Sauvignon Blanc 2004
Marlborough
New Zealand

When it comes to NZ Sauvignon Blanc, local winemaking dynamo Matt Thompson is "the man".

Responsible for a swag of Marlborough's slickest examples, it's Thompson's Mudhouse Sauvignon Blanc that most recently rocked my world. And all the usual suspects are here too: gooseberry, elderflower, and blackcurrant slung together with the kind of mouth-watering acidity that just keeps you reaching for more.

Dangerously awesome…

Knappstein
Hand Picked Riesling 2004
South Australia
Australia

For as long as I've been working in wine (and that's nudging twelve years), a Riesling comeback has been threatening to take the planet's wine consumers by the short and curlies. And to some degree it has, although when you line up the world's greatest Riesling alongside say the world's greatest Chardonnay – the difference in price is frightening…

The bottom line is that great Riesling is still good value, and this wine is a cracker. Super limey and complete with racy acid and a spankingly dry finish.

Merlonay
April 1 2005, 11.59pm

A revolution is about to take place in wine shops the world over and Merlonay is the star of the show. It seems the wider drinking public are about to be possessed by a new variety that will surely re-shape the face of the wine industry as we've come to know it.

A very deliberate and genetically modified cross of red grape Merlot and white grape Chardonnay (and having just produced a lazy 9.5 million hectolitres from the 2004 vintage thanks to scientists "juicing up" its yielding potential), Merlonay is now the most feverishly planted grape, and soon to be most consumed variety, on earth.

It seems that the wine community at large is right behind the variety too. T-shirts with the slogan "It's OK to drink Merlonay" and "Merlonay is here to stay" are at present time strewn across much of winemaking California – Merlonay's spiritual home! And with the announcement this week that Merlonay will have it's very own category at next months prestigious Cellarman World Wine Awards, it seems that the notoriously sceptical wine media also see a long-term future in this variety.

So what does it taste like then?

Merlonay appears white, but tastes red (perfect for those of you who don't like the fact that red wine stains your teeth!). Characteristically, classic examples will smell and taste sweet and fruity, with a slightly animal edge.

Also, Merlonay is naturally high in tannin and acidity, but genetic modification has meant that the wine appears soft, juicy, and without any "major dryness" – how great is that!

Thumbs up for Merlonay I say!

Stonecroft
Syrah 2001
Hawke's Bay
New Zealand

get it from…

United Kingdom
£12.95

Lea & Sandeman

I'll probably get my citizenship revoked for saying this, but New Zealand is home to some of the most exciting examples of Syrah (Shiraz) around in the New World.

Where these wines differ from those of their Aussie neighbours is first and foremost in the alcohol and oak department. A "less-is-more" approach has resulted in wines that rely on fruit and oak as only two parts of a bigger equation.

Following in the footsteps of the awesome Kingsley Estate and the consistently good Te Mata "Bullnose", this wine is an essay in blackberry, plum, fresh ground pepper, and allspice. Nab some if you see it.

Palliser
Pinot Noir 2002
Martinborough
New Zealand

get it from…

United Kingdom
£12.99

Philglass & Swiggot

Outside of France, Pinot Noir has found few places to really call home. And while Australia and the USA continue to get their heads around this variety, New Zealand has been off and running for some time now and is currently in the process of kicking some major goals with Pinot.

Hailing from Martinborough (think southern tip of the North Island), this wine has it all – beautiful aromatics lead to velvet-like texture and great length of flavour, both of which are neatly woven together by some very tidy super-fine tannin. A very sexy beast indeed.

Biblia Chora
Red 2002
Macedonia
Greece

Screwcaps, posh new wineries, great international press – even the first Greek Master of Wine, have all been the result of a very deliberate twenty-year Herculean push to haul Greece's wine industry into modern times.

You'll find all the usual suspects here, too: Cabernet Sauvignon, Syrah, Chardonnay, and Viognier are right at home alongside less familiar local varieties such as Assyrtiko, Malagousia, and Agiorgitiko.

Relying on international travellers Cabernet and Merlot for its stuffing, this wine – loaded with dark spicy fruit – would proudly walk tall in the company of similar new world styles at twice the money.

get it from…

United Kingdom
£6.99

Waitrose
Majestic

Yalumba
Merlot 2003
South Australia
Australia

If ever there was a wine that spelt out in simple terms what this variety is all about, it's the insanely consistent Yalumba Merlot.

Loaded with aromas and flavours of dark plum, sweet spice, and chocolate, this wine is sweet, soft, and warm – kind of like your favourite blanket. Apart from being awesome value for money, this is such a great place to kick start a love affair with red wine.

Green Point
"ZD" NV
South Australia
Australia

get it from…

United Kingdom
£10.00

Waitrose
Philglass & Swiggot

A few steps back in the process before a cork is stuffed in, all fizzy wine produced by the "traditional method" begins life under a crown seal (think beer bottle top).

The team behind Moët's Aussie arm Green Point should all be given awards for bravery for being the first to commercially release such a radical and obvious seal. Not a smidge of cork in sight, eliminating any chance of all that clean appley, citrus-like fizz being spoilt. With such a good wine, they won't be the last.

Pretty in Pink
June 11 2005, 11.57pm

The Camilla Thomas and Audrey Gregor issue – otherwise known as the new Aussie babies! xx

Pink stinks!

God how I wish I had a pound or a dollar for every time I said that as a schoolboy who didn't know better. Anyway, nearly twenty years on the irony is that pink still stinks, but only in a good way! You see one of my favourite Champagnes, Billecart-Salmon Rosé, is pink and it smells amazing! My all-time favorite meal – dim sum – is never better than paired up with pink wine. And, when I'm really really thirsty, a nice big glass of super-cold pale-pink wine seems to hit the spot like nothing else on earth.

Regular weekly "Juice" readers will now probably realize that I have a good old-fashioned obsession with rosé. Whether or not my obsession is classed as unhealthy is debatable, but, you see, I reckon that rosé is good for you. Think about it. Rosé tends to get drunk when the sun's out – sun is good for you. The very thought of drinking rosé makes people smile – smiling is also good for you. Science boffins like Jimmy will be elated to know that rosé contains tannin. Tannin – a natural antioxidant – is a polyphenol. Polyphenols help to lower both cholesterol and blood pressure, stimulate the immune system, and – we think – help protect your body against "The Big C", and well if that's not good for you… Now I'm no rocket scientist, but mix all of that together and you should end up with a triple dose of goodness.

How good is that! Not the world's most logical justification for "wine being good for you", I know, but who cares, it's just wine – pink wine to be precise! Enjoy it.

Falesco
Vitiano 2002
Umbria
Italy

get it from…

United Kingdom
£8.49

Oddbins

One of the serious contenders for *The Juice* wine of the year, this red has everything you would want and expect from an Italian beauty costing twice as much.

Pieced together by consultant winemaker extraordinaire Ricardo Cottarella, Falesco (Cotarella's own estate) Vittiano is a soft and extremely gluggable blend of Cabernet Sauvignon, Sangiovese, and Merlot that is just longing for your attention!

United Kingdom
£8.99

Philglass & Swiggot
Valvona & Crolla

Planeta
La Segreta 2004
Sicily
Italy

It's almost like the sky's the limit for this hugely popular Sicilian estate. And right at the front of the stable is the deliciously drinkable La Segreta Rosso.

A chunky, fruit-driven mix of Cabernet, Merlot, and the local Nero d'Avola, you can hold your head high as you present this to your dad-in-law-to-be and say "Tuscany is so yesterday – the south is where it's happening!"

get it from…

United Kingdom
£6.99 (37.5cl)

Philglass & Swiggot

Campbells of Rutherglen
Muscat NV
Victoria
Australia

Rutherglen in northeastern Victoria produces some of the most amazing and unique sweet wines from anywhere in the world.

Super rich and concentrated, these wines are made using heavily raisined grapes. And although production methods are many and varied, the raisins are squeezed for what little juice they contain. Then natural spirit is added to capture and preserve all that beautiful juice and prohibit fermentation.

Think aromas of toffee and molasses, Middle Eastern spices, nuts, and dried fruits and you get the picture. A meal in itself, but great after a dinner served with cheese and maybe even a few blocks of chocolate. Oh go on!

Valdespino
Pedro Ximenez El Candado NV
Jerez
Spain

get it from…

United Kingdom
£11.50

Lea & Sandeman

Pedro Ximenez (*pedro-him-en-eth*), or PX, is a sort of "tricky to say/ very easy to drink" Spanish grape variety native to the sherry region in the country's south.

Widely available, great examples of PX are almost black in colour, incredibly syrupy and super sweet, with intense aromas of raisins, dried fruits, coffee, and spice. The best way to drink PX is after dinner drizzled over vanilla ice-cream, or by the glass with a slice or three of nanna's fruit cake.

You don't have to drink it all in one go – this should last you six weeks once you've cracked it open, but I bet it doesn't!

Kooyung
Pinot Noir 2001
Victoria
Australia

get it from…

United Kingdom
£15.95

Lea & Sandeman

Kooyong winemaker Sandro Mosele is a gun. Having spent his apprenticeship under the watchful eyes of some of Australia's greatest producers, Mosele has kicked some monster goals at this small property on Victoria's Mornington Peninsula.

Scratch through the cedary surface and find a whole box full of wild fruits, dark cherry, and sweet spice. Meanwhile in your mouth it's silky and fine with bright fruit and a gentle wash of super-fine tannin – one of the real hallmarks of this variety.

Buy a few bottles, forget about them then pat yourself on the back a few years from now when you find them again! Awesome.

get it from…

United Kingdom
£9.99

Waitrose
Liberty Wines

Shaw and Smith
Sauvignon Blanc 2004
South Australia
Australia

This is easily the best Sauvignon Blanc in Australia and takes its quality right up to the best their neighbours across the pond (NZ) have to offer.

Any paler and it would faint, this wine very elegantly steps out of the glass, slaps you across the face and says "what the *£@# are you waiting for? Drink me now!" All the usual suspects are here too: passion-fruit, elderflower, fresh spring peas – all of which are bound up in one very slick package.

get it from…

United Kingdom
£10.95

The Wine Society

Trimbach
Gewurztraminer 2003
Alsace
France

Sadly, Gewurztraminer probably takes the prize for being the uncoolest grape variety in the world.

In reality though, Gewurz is one of the superstar varieties of Alsace located in France's northeastern corner, and Trimbach is one of the area's finest producers.

As far as aromas and flavours go Gewurz would go down as one of the more interesting grape varieties around. Oozing smells of lychee, orange blossom, ginger, and spice, the palate is rich and oily with low acidity and great length of flavour.

Cape Mentelle
Semillon/Sauvignon Blanc 2004
South Australia
Australia

get it from…

United Kingdom
£10.99

Waitrose

This was the bottle I was holding
on a wine/surf road trip to Margaret
River a few years ago, when one
of my best mates Thommo casually
wandered into the wine shop and
told me that "the fact our hire car
has just plummeted down the hill
and smashed into the back of
another parked vehicle might just
have something to do with you
leaving the handbrake off and not
putting the car in gear?!" Ooops,
that'll teach me…

I've long been a fan of this wine.
Simple, but spotlessly clean, citrus
and stone fruit is the theme both
on the nose and in the mouth,
while a long and balanced drying
finish wraps it up nicely.

TV
Dinners

Wines to have with Friday night take-away

A huge chunk of my day is spent talking to people about food and wine, but rarely does this mirror how I eat and drink at home. Here I offer pure and simple matches that work, bringing together affordable wine (at around a tenner) and food combinations rather than the kind we dream about. If you're even the faintest bit handy in the kitchen, or a take-away fanatic – then there's a wine here to compliment. Take a look, you don't have to make a meal of it. Bon Appetite!

Banrock Station
Sparkling Shiraz NV
South Australia
Australia

get it from…

United Kingdom
£7.99

Waitrose

OK, if you've never experienced a mouthful of sparkling red before then you'll have to work with me here. Picture a big, rich, chunky red wine – only picture it fizzy and served cold! Sounds good?

With most relying on Shiraz as the star variety of choice, the additional hint of sweetness and a good dose of tannin means that in all but a few cases, these are wines that should work brilliantly with any food that is sweet, salty, sour, hot, or sticky.

Frothy, purple (try not to spill it on the carpet please) and bursting with aromas of sweet plum, blackberry jam, and dark chocolate – alongside "Skinner's Killer Ribs" (find the recipe at www.lovewinedrinkbetter.com) you're laughing.

William Fèvre
Petit Chablis 2003
Burgundy
France

get it from…
United Kingdom
£10.99

Waitrose

If you ever needed a crystal-clear illustration of regional influence, then stop at the great-big patchwork quilt that is France's Chablis district.

With the best vineyards sitting snug on top of Kimmeridgian limestone that dates back to the Jurassic era (over 150 million years ago!), Chablis produces wines made from Chardonnay, and mainly without the influence of oak.

Typically these wines are squeaky clean and minerally as if you've just taken a slurp from the freshest stream on earth. Aromas and flavours are of lemon, honeysuckle, and chalk – all of which make this style of wine perfect with the biggest plate of fresh-shucked oysters you can lay your hands on!

Completely Screwed
June 18 2004, 1.17pm

Bit of a serious Juice this week I'm afraid. Unless you've been living in a bubble (Chris Terry and Michael Jackson) for the past few years, you might already be aware of the super-sized debate that's been simmering away over the pros and cons of the screwcap (*a.k.a.* Stelvin closure) versus the cork. Sad I know, but it's big news in my world and it affects you too – so listen up!

It's estimated that between five and seven per cent of all wine bottled with a traditional cork ends up being ruined by a type of bacteria known as TCA – every winemaker's worst nightmare. And with the current rate of around one dud bottle in fifteen, the efforts of cork manufactures to clean up their act are a matter of too little too late. The effect of random oxidation (premature ageing of a wine due to oxygen contact) is even harder to measure.

Winemakers have explored nearly every possible avenue to identify something better than a cork. Enter the screwcap. Romantic they're not – but then again neither are seat belts and you still wear one of those! Screwcaps guarantee that your wine will 99.9 per cent taste as the winemaker intended it to. Now surely that's a good thing?

So, with the screwcap phenomenon continuing to spread across the planet, resistance from Old World producers is strong. Kind of ironic considering the screwcap was in fact a French invention? Dig a bit deeper and you stumble across a major hurdle here in London.

As one of the world's most important wine markets, London's wine scene is largely controlled by European sommeliers and wine buyers – who just ain't sold on screwcaps. And if the key holders of the planet's largest wine purse ain't sold then the producer ain't sold either. Get it?

Poggerino
Il Labirinto 2000
Tuscany
Italy

Native red Tuscan superstar Sangiovese is a variety that many people can find tough going if they're not used to the excessively drying tannins that are a hallmark of this style. But, paired up with the right food, say something relatively oily like pizza, and presto, you're in food and wine heaven. Well, my kind of heaven that is!

In true Tuscan style, Il Labirinto – hammered together by the super talented Pierro Lanza – displays lifted dark-cherry fruit alongside aromas of tobacco, earth, and spice. In your mouth it's soft and rich, finishing with a wash of those above-mentioned super drying tannins.

get it from…

United Kingdom
£13.00

Philglass & Swiggot

Bowen Estate
Cabernet Sauvignon 2000
South Australia
Australia

If lamb – particularly the nice, sweet, juicy, chargrilled kind – is on the menu then a decent bottle of Cabernet is a must rather than a maybe. Coonawarra without Cabernet would be like Siegfried without Roy, Bert without Ernie, C3-PO without R2…

Local producer, Bowen Estate is amongst the region's finest, and the wines simply ooze class. This example is big, red, and bang full of sun-drenched fruit. On board you'll find aromas of cassis, blood plum, leather, and mint, while the palate is choc full of sweet-dark fruit and some trademark Cabernet drying tannin. Nab some while you can!

United Kingdom
£9.00

Waitrose
Majestic
Bibendum

Catena
Chardonnay 2003
Mendoza
Argentina

Chardonnay is pretty much happy sinking its roots anywhere. The real challenge with Chardonnay lies not in the growing, but in the way it's produced.

Pitched in the foothills of the Andes mountains, Catena has produced an example that's packed full of sweet-grapefruit citrus flavours and grilled hazelnut aromas.

The end result is a wine that should automatically have you reaching for a nice big chicken, a handful of fresh thyme, half a lemon, a good old glug of olive oil, a roasting tin, and a nice hot oven. Away you go!

Hewitson
Riesling 2004
South Australia
Australia

Easily one of the hottest producers in Oz right now, Dean Hewitson is a master when it comes to crafting wines using fruit sourced from a super-select bunch of South Australia's best grape growers.

The wines are really well priced, too, not to mention extremely versatile with a stack of different food styles. In this case the Hewitson Riesling comes packing trademark citrus punch, spice, and biscuity aromas. The palate is rich, limey, and bone-dry – a lethal combination with a fresh Thai take-out.

get it from…

United Kingdom
£9.99

Robersons
Berry Bros & Rudd

Perrin et Fils
Châteauneuf-du-Pape
Les Sinards 2001
Rhône
France

get it from…

United Kingdom
£15.00

Waitrose
Berry Bros & Rudd

Perrin is the parent company and (much more affordable) second label of Southern Rhône superstar, Beaucastel.

Drawing on organically grown Grenache (with Mourvèdre and Syrah making up numbers) it is largely assembled from declassified Beaucastel fruit.

So, not only do you get serious bang for your buck here, but this wine is nothing short of an essay in chunky dark fruit, and rustic Châteauneuf spice. As a rule, slow cooked casseroles – the ones that have all that sticky meat and those delicious rich cooking juices – absolutely rock with these kinds of wines.

get it from…

United Kingdom
£8.99

Robersons

Viña Rodríguez
Dehesa Gago 2003
Toro
Spain

Hot from the stable of one of Spain's brightest young wine stars comes this insanely priced un-wooded Tempranillo. Relying heavily on a solid core of dark cherry and bright, raspberry fruit, the palate is clean, fresh, soft, and a total pleasure to drink.

The fact that the wine hasn't seen a whisker of oak means you might match it up with dishes that would otherwise have been a bit light.

Apart from being one of my favourite meals, Mrs Skins' char-grilled chorizo sandwich – complete with peppery rocket and garlicky aioli – makes for a killer combination with Dehesa. Delicious!

Pot Luck
March 16 2005, 1.22pm

As an Aussie I come with an inherent condition that forces me into a complete and utter frenzy over most types of sport. Football, cricket, tennis, swimming, rugby (although we're still not talking about that), darts, even lawn bowls – you name it and I'll find a way to jump up and down on the couch, shout at the television, and love it!

So those of you who share my illness can probably imagine my sense of excitement when I was taken to my first game of British football a few years back. Chelsea v Aston Villa – promised to be a good game too, but God it was boring. Sorry, just three goals were scored in two hours of play, and no one bled. Where's the "jump up and down" excitement in that? As a result I've been forced to find comfort in that "other" British sport… Snooker.

Complete with it's own breed of heroes – Steve Davis, Jimmy "The Whirlwind" White, and Paul Hunter (the Jamie Oliver of snooker?!) – snooker's got me hook, line.

Just in case you missed it, "Rocket" Ronnie O'Sullivan – snooker's equivalent to Michael Schumacher (and my fave player) – won the Masters on Sunday in one of the most devastating displays of skill to be witnessed on the green cloth. Versatile, precise, and silky – yet powerful and concentrated when required – if Ronnie were a grape, he'd simply have to be Pinot Noir.

Colourful adjectives aside Pinot Noir is generally considered the lightest of the red grape family, which means if you're not a huge fan of great big reds then Pinot Noir could be the one for you! But it's a tricky, low-yielding variety that only likes particular climates, so you might just have to pay a bit more than usual to have "your mind blown".

Pieropan
Soave Classico 2004
Soave
Italy

get it from…

United Kingdom
£8.99

Philglas & Swiggot
Liberty Wines

Spaghetti with garlic, salt, pepper, and whatever olive oil you can afford is one of the greatest "budget conscious" dishes on the planet. On snow-boarding holidays where cash was always limited, my best mate Tobie would cook this dish for us day in day out – adding things like chilli, lemon, parmesan, capers or anchovies for variation. My job was the wine.

Unlike a lot of Soave, this wine has both style and substance. Delicate and light with plenty of fresh pear and apple character, Pieropan is a complete winner with any spaghetti combination you choose. Even though we were always the scruffiest kids in the chalet, there was nothing shabby about the way we ate and drank!

A-Mano
Primitivo 2003
Puglia
Italy

get it from…

United Kingdom
£5.99

Booths
Liberty Wines

The south of Italy is on the rise. Areas like Puglia, Sardinia, and Sicily are on fire and hammering out some really great examples – particularly in the "big and red" category.

The best thing about many of these wines is that, because of a super warm climate, the wines end up stuffed full of fruit, with a softness that lends itself to early drinking. On a recent trip down south I lived on penne with tomato, tuna, olives, capers, and chilli – a complete and utter winner with this stonkingly good-value wine from Puglia stars, A-Mano.

get it from…

United Kingdom
£8.99

Berkmann Wine Cellars

Grover Vineyards
La Réserve 2002
Bangalore
India

One of the things I enjoy most about my job is all the amazing discoveries I make along the way. Indian wine (yes, India!) was a total revelation.

Grover Vineyards is India's first bonafide wine-producing superstar. And while they haven't quite hit the dizzying heights of others around the globe, they're having a good old crack – something definitely worth supporting.

Michel Rolland is the consultant winemaker here, and for that and many other reasons this soft, spicy blend of Shiraz and Cabernet is well worth a look alongside a couple of juicy tandoori lamb chops.

Delta Vineyard
Pinot Noir 2004
Marlborough
New Zealand

Marlborough's long, flat valley floors (northern end of New Zealand's South Island) are home to world-class Sauvignon Blanc, but more recently all the fun's been had in the hills where red grape Pinot Noir has kicked some serious goals.

Breaking the NZ mould, Delta is less about big fruit, and more about purity and finesse – both of which make this a killer wine to have with food styles that run along similar lines. Think Japanese – in particular, tuna or salmon sashimi – and you'll definitely be on the right track.

Hugel
Pinot Blanc 2004
Alsace
France

get it from…

United Kingdom
£11.95

The Wine Society

While Pinot Blanc rarely, if ever, swims in the same league as the great Riesling, Gewurztraminer, and Pinot Gris, it's definitely the underrated quiet achiever of Alsace in France. And it's easy to see why.

Aromas of white peach, fresh flowers, talc, and minerals set you up for a mouthful of wine that tastes just as good as it sounds.

Fish tacos are a bit of a staple in our house, and the combination of soft shell tacos, char-grilled salmon, spicy guacamole, and fresh salsa beg for a wine with simple and uncomplicated flavours. Hugel Pinot Blanc is right up to that task.

McWine
June 25 2004, 12.08pm

Surely in the wake of last week's three times 100,000-strong sell-out Hyde Park gigs in London, the Red Hot Chilli Peppers are not only one of the hottest bands in the galaxy right now, but arguably one of California's better recent export successes. From Disney to Dogtown through to Hollywood and Hamburgers, California has given us plenty, but the one area where she continues to fall short is in the wine department, and we're talking grand scale with capital GS.

Walk into any corner wine store and within seconds flat you're bound to be accosted by a bargain basement wall of Blossom Hill, Ernst & Julio Gallo or – scarier still – both!

Even more frightening is the statistic that each year, "goliath-like" Californian producer Gallo single-handedly churns out more wine than Australia's combined total production. Would you like fries with that? It's all beginning to sound very familiar…

At the opposite end of the scale, the problem is that top-end wine from the really great Californian producers is either spat out in such microscopic quantities that it barely touches the sides, or, it simply ends up way too expensive for Joe Average (you and me!).

Of course there are exceptions to the rule – good people doing great wine at sensible prices – and California has its fair share of them, just be prepared to have to hunt them out!

Tamar Ridge
Pinot Noir 2002
Tasmania
Australia

get it from…

United Kingdom
£10.95

Lay & Wheeler

Pinot Noir and duck share an affinity for one another that sees them comfortably sit side-by-side in food-and-wine's Hall of Fame. Pinot can be many things, but works best when it has enough sweet fruit to stack up against the flavour of duck, some nice spice-and-earth character to offset the gaminess of the bird, and super-fine tannin to clean your palate having just chewed and swallowed a mouthful of meat.

Making great Pinot for under a tenner is a very hard job. But the gang at Tamar have risen to the challenge, and done it well. The nose is packed with bright, raspberry, cherry, and cinnamon aromas, while the palate is plummy, soft, and supported well by a wash of mega-fine tannins.

get it from…

United Kingdom
£8.99 (50cl)

Adnams
Noel Young Wines

Viña Rodríguez
MR Moscatel 2003
Malaga
Spain

With Spain currently in the midst of a major wine revolution, you can be assured of hearing plenty more about the current man of the hour, Telmo Rodríguez (*see also* p.10).

With a handful of (mainly red) stellar examples from Rodríguez currently gracing the shelves of good wine stores worldwide, it's his sweet wine from Malaga (of all places) which continues to blow my mind.

Jam-packed with aromas of sweet-orange rind, apple, and mint, this wine does its best work in your mouth, where it displays concentrated pear and honeyed fruit and a super long, expansive finish.

Bound to be a hit with the tarts – lemon, that is!

get it from…

United Kingdom
£5.99

Liberty Wines
Andrew Chapman Fine
Wines

Quatroventi
Rosato 2003
Puglia
Italy

Weekly "Juice" readers will more than likely already know about the absurd value that is A-Mano Primitivo, quite possibly one of Italy's – if not the planet's – best value reds.

The latest incarnation from the team at A-Mano comes in the form of Quatroventi – a bone dry, ultra-refreshing, stonkingly good rosato made from southern Italian varieties Malvasia Nera and Negroamaro.

Essential summer drinking with a great big salad of sweet juicy tomatoes, super fresh mozzarella, and a handful of basil leaves.

Allegrini
Valpolicella 2003
Valpolicella
Italy

get it from…

United Kingdom
£7.99

Philglass & Swiggot

Simply put, Allegrini are to grapes what Ferrari are to cars. For decades this Valpolicella-based family has refined it's product in a bid to make the very best wines it can.

At the top of the tree the Amarone is unmatched, while the single-vineyard La Poja is among Italy's great reds. The basic Valpolicella Classico – officially the world's best roast-pork sandwich wine – reeks of Allegrini style, but thankfully comes without the scary price tag. So fresh it almost glows, the nose delivers lifted raspberry and sweet, dark cherry fruit while in the mouth its medium-bodied, soft, and delicious.

Wine Time Viewing
March 18 2005, 2.23pm

I finally saw *Sideways* at the weekend (more about that on p.38). I liked it, too. Enjoyable scriptwriting, good characters, and definitely not treading near *A Walk in the Clouds* territory – that highly forgettable Hollywood wine flick that Keanu "no way dude" Reeves starred in a few years back.

But, the thing I really liked about *Sideways* was that it had been well researched from a wine point of view. Pinot Noir gets a proper bigging up, Sauvignon Blanc scores public approval, and Merlot cops a good old-fashioned beating (more on that on another page) – there's even a few nice *Trainspotting* moments for those of you seriously "in the know".

References to '88 Sassicaia, '61 Cheval Blanc, DRC Richebourg, and the "We even drank it with artichokes and didn't care" comment should be enough to keep most wine bores (sadly) elbowing those closest to them in acknowledgement (sorry Carls). But the *piéce de resistance* has to be the Oscar-worthy "spit bucket" scene toward the movie's end – a truly priceless moment!

Wine's answer to *Easyrider* it's not, but as a loveable, low budget film about a two mates on a wine road trip through California's stunning Santa Barbara County, it's well worth a visit. Hire it out (don't go to see it as it's obviously long finished in cinemas).

d'Arenberg
d'Arry's Original 2002
South Australia
Australia

get it from…

United Kingdom
£8.69

Booths
Bibendum

Since 1943, d'Arry Osborne has firmly focused his attention on handcrafting some of the most high-quality examples of Grenache and Syrah produced anywhere in the New World. In saying that, one of the most endearing qualities of d'Arenberg is that as consistently good as the wines are – and that's very good – they continue to remain affordable and this producer has never lost sight of its market.

This wine is a 50/50 blend of Grenache and Shiraz that literally explodes with sweet-dark fruit the moment you stick your nose into the glass. It's designed to drink young and preferably alongside a couple of your favourite sausages and a great big plate of mash!

United Kingdom
£9.95

Berry Bros & Rudd

Escudo
Rojo 2002
Maipo
Chile

As the Chilean love-child of
Bordeaux superpower Baron
Philippe de Rothschild, this wine
has some pretty big boots to fill
if it's to cut the mustard in this family.

Chileans love their meat, and just
to prove that some of the greatest
food and wine combinations on the
planet are also some of the simplest,
pull the cork on a bottle of Escudo,
wrap your hands around the very
best burger you know of, and see
the light!

Yarra Bank
Cuvée 1999
Victoria
Australia

As a rule the words "good", "cheap", and "sparkling" rarely walk hand in hand in hand. Champagne house Devaux are just one of a growing number of producers who have invested sizably in Australia's cooler states. Devaux's reward is the really, really good Yarra Bank Brut, and the current release (1999) is a beauty.

Incorporating Chardonnay, Pinot Noir, and Pinot Meunier, this wine consistently rates as one of my favourite cheaper-end fizzies – not to mention one half of one of my best homesickness remedies – Champagne/sparkling wine and fish and chips!

Home brand. Hmmm…

I can't help feeling just a touch suspicious when I cross paths with "own-label" products in the supermarket – especially when it comes to wine.

I guess my suspicion stems from the fact that history has seen more than its fair share of unsavory scammers – who, through a mix of "brand strength" and consumer ignorance, have abused own-label wine products in order to facilitate their own large-scale profiteering.

Hmmm… But as Bob would say, "times they are a changing" and as a general rule, supermarket "own labels" have never been in better shape. In fact, I'd even go as far as to say that if you're shopping for wine around at lower price points, then supermarket own-labels are once again very safe territory.

And with a pinch above seventy per cent of all wine purchased in the UK done so in supermarkets, they definitely don't want to see you buy your wine elsewhere. So, in order to keep you happy, "petrol pirates" have been replaced with crack teams of "Schwarzenegger-style" wine commandos (well, that might be a slight exaggeration) who are paid by supermarkets to scour the earth in a bid to help you drink better – and most importantly – cheaper!

I've lined up a ton of them this week – well, a few anyway – and I have to say that in general I was blown-away by the overall quality of what's on offer, all of which just goes to prove that you should never judge a book by its cover!

Jermann
Pinot Bianco 2003
Friuli-Venezia Giulia
Italy

get it from…

United Kingdom
£10.25

Valvona & Crolla

Silvio Jermann is one of the greatest white wine producers in the world. His legendary "Dreams" Chardonnay (of which he only ever made eight vintages) rates as one of the most collectable white wines ever to come out of Italy.

Die-hard fans however, will tell you that the wine not to miss out on is "Vintage Tunina" – an eclectic mix of Chardonnay, Sauvignon Blanc, and Picolit. That's all great, but our fave wine from the funky man of Friuli is the insanely cheap Pinot Bianco.

Made from the variety of the same name, this wine is clean, light, lemony and not to be missed with a great big bowl of spaghetti vongole. *Belissimo*!

Teruzzi & Puthod
Vernaccia di San Gimignano 2004
Tuscany
Italy

get it from…

United Kingdom
£8.95

Valvona & Crolla
Berkmann Wine Cellars

Hard to pronounce, mega-easy to drink! This wine, made from summery, Tuscan white grape Vernaccia, is a super-clean and well-made example from San Gimignano in central Italy.

With aromas and flavours of honeysuckle, pear, apple, and minerals, this is great-value summer drinking at its best; and bound to be a big hit with grilled fish, a wedge of lemon, and a nice old glug of new-season olive oil.

get it from…

United Kingdom
£9.00

Bibendum

Huia
Gewurztraminer 2004
Marlborough
New Zealand

This wine hails from Marlborough at the northern end of New Zealand's South Island where some insanely good wine – mainly made from aromatic white varieties – is made.

Made from Gewurztraminer, expect a tightly wound nose of rosewater, musk, lychee, and ginger. And while Gewurz is more often my weapon of choice to take to our nearby Vietnamese, wines like this will really rise to the occasion when paired with assorted steamed dumplings, all the usual deep-fried suspects, glutinous rice, slippery hand-stretched noodles, and a cast of sauces – hot, sour, sweet, and salty.

Gaia
Notios 2000
Santorini
Greece

Greek wine is on the up and – although there's still a truckload of work to be done – most of the examples currently available to us on the high street are really well made and more importantly, super good value for money.

If you're into soft, fruity reds then check out this stunner from the island of Santorini. Made from local variety Agiorgitiko (don't try to say it, just drink it), this wine is bright, with plenty of dark-currant and plum-like fruit and a nice spicy edge. The perfect candidate for char-grilled lamb souvlaki (easy on the garlic sauce tiger!).

Bound to become a new barbeque classic.

Frescobaldi
Rèmole 2003
Tuscany
Italy

Sweet, lush, and forward, this super-lovable wine from Frescobaldi is made from a blend of Merlot and Sangiovese – the native red superstar of Tuscany.

Packed with aromas and flavours of dense dark cherry, tobacco, earth, and spice, it's the sweet inky fruit and wash of trademark dry grippy tannins that will serve this wine so well alongside a nice big char-grilled piece of steak.

Bling

When money is no object, or someone else is paying!

You're dripping in gold and rolling in a fresh pair of trainers every time you step out. Or, maybe the boss has carelessly given you the company card to look after the wine at today's business lunch. In this chapter we've thrown caution to the wind and tossed the budget out the window. Some of the prices are enough to make your eyes water, but I can guarantee that each of the following gems is worth every single penny.

get it from…

United Kingdom
£13.00

Sainsbury's

Majella
Cabernet Sauvignon 2003
South Australia
Australia

Over the years, Majella has carved out some super-fine examples of Cabernet Sauvignon. These wines are not only high quality, but perhaps more importantly offer a crystal clear snapshot of Coonawarra.

Focused cassis and blood plum with hints of leather and mint are all evident on the nose, while the palate is concentrated and choc full of sweet fruit and firm drying tannins. 2002 was a tip-top vintage for Coonawarra. Check it out.

Poderi Aldo Conterno
Barolo 1998
Piedmont
Italy

get it from…

United Kingdom
£36.00

Four Walls Wine Co.
Classic & Rare Wine Ltd

Let's just say that if heaven turns
out to be anything like Piedmont,
then that's completely cool with
me. Home to red varieties like
Barbera and Dolcetto, it's the
temperamental superstar, Nebbiolo,
that rules the roost, consistently
cranking out some of the most
seductive, intriguing, and sexy wines
assembled anywhere on the planet.

This wine is made from 100%
Nebbiolo and has all the hallmarks
of Conterno's Midas touch. The
nose has classic trademark aromas
of dark cherry, fresh roses, black
olives, tobacco, earth, and exotic
spices. Drink it now with a really
good piece of lamb or stick it away
for the next few years if you can
manage to!

Almaviva
2001
Maipo
Chile

Chile's first real super wine (and surely not its last), is the result of a joint venture between Baron Philippe de Rothschild of France and Chilean wine superpower, Concha y Toro.

Cabernet is the star performer in Almaviva delivering insane intensity, structure, and charm. It's all here too. Ripe cassis, fresh liquorice straps, my favourite leather jacket, cedar, and sweet spice. Half the fun is watching this monster unwind in the glass – an indication that it will more than likely benefit from a few years in a cool, dark spot somewhere near you!

Alvaro Palacios
Les Terrasses 2001
Priorat
Spain

With all the drama you might expect from a good episode of *Dynasty*, the Alvaro Palacios story is a great one – it even comes with a happy ending. Now back in charge of the family estate, Palacios Remondo, in Rioja, it's Alvaro's own wines that continue to turn heads around the planet.

We're talking about a very talented young winemaker – the star pupil of Christian Moueix no less. This wine comes off the steep vineyards of Priorat. It's inky, rich, and powerful with masses of ripe fruit due to the blending of vineyards (some 100 years old) and varieties – Cariñena, Granacha, Cabernet Sauvignon, and Syrah to be exact. Handle with care.

Terroirism
July 30 2004, 1.07pm

Somewhereness. I've just learnt a new word. Seriously, it's a proper word – go to www.wordspy.com and look it up if you don't believe me!

So what does it mean and what's it got to do with wine? Well, somewhereness happens to be one of those new "too cool for school" words that means much the same thing as the French word, "terroir" (*te-wah*). And what's terroir? Well, that's slightly harder to explain, as it doesn't really have a straightforward English translation.

In a nutshell, terroir is more of a concept that ultimately defines the identity of a place – or in the case of wine, a plot of land. Sun, soil, sea, wind, rain, plants, animals, people, my football team (well maybe not), the universe, the galaxy – all of these and more, much much more – will have a massive impact on how a particular wine from a particular place will end up tasting. It's regionalism on steroids. *Comprenez-vous*? This is terroir.

However, not all wines are reflective of their origins, and nor do they have to be. Many big companies who are churning out frightening volumes of wine, are often forced to source grapes from a number of different areas – even countries – ultimately wiping out any trace of regional influence. This is known as multi-regional blending, and it's not a bad thing so long as the wines are good.

Me, I like wines that taste of where they're from. Part of me enjoys the idea that these wines represent "a year in the life of somewhere". The other part likes the fact that they're a true test of a winemaker's skill depending on what Mother Nature decides to dish up. Even in the dodgiest of years, great winemakers will still make good wines – wines that taste of somewhereness!

get it from…

United Kingdom
£25.99

Noel Young Wines

Ata Rangi
Pinot Noir 2001
Martinborough
New Zealand

For the past decade Ata Rangi has set the standard for New Zealand Pinot Noir. Its wines are magically crafted, layered, complex, and, best of all, built to go the distance.

Watching them unwind in the glass is amazing. From bright dark-cherry and plum-like fruit to aromas of earth, spice, and truffle, these are consistently amongst my favourite wines in the world.

Buy a few, try one now and stick the rest under the bed for the next three to five years.

Au Bon Climat
Chardonnay 2002
California
USA

get it from…

United Kingdom
£14.95

Berry Bros & Rudd

Sporting one of the world's better mullets, Au Bon Climat owner-winemaker Jim Clendenen also happens to posses the Midas touch when it comes to producing world-class examples of both Chardonnay and Pinot Noir.

In the case of this wine, we're talking about a stunning California Chardonnay dressed up in French clothes. Subtle, elegant, and way to sexy for it's own good, this wine is special occasion stuff that will blow the mind of anybody you pour it for. Way to go Jim.

Château de Beaucastel
Châteauneuf-du-Pape 2002
Rhône
France

It's difficult to put into words just
how good this estate is. Owned
by the Rhône-based Perrin brothers,
Beaucastel is one of Châteauneuf-
du-Pape's star performers.

Predominantly Grenache, but
pieced together from a mix of
all thirteen permitted varieties
in the region, this wine is an essay
in complexity.

Organics play a huge role here too,
and layer-upon-layer of fruit, spice,
earth, and farmyard aromas unwind
and lead you to flavours that just
go on and on and on in your mouth.
The tannins are fine, the acidity
well-balanced, and all in all, this
is one of the world's great wines.

Prager
Grüner Veltliner 2002
Wachau
Austria

get it from…

United Kingdom
£21.95

Berry Bros & Rudd

Not content with having just thrust Austria's wine scene back into the limelight, Grüner Veltliner has wooed wine-lovers right around the planet in true pied-piper-like fashion. With a foot in the "full-bodied and white" camp, expect to smell an exotic and exhausting range of things from ripe tropical fruit, pears, and grapefruit through to pepper, spice, and wet wool.

Prager is one of Austria's finest Grüner (and Riesling) producers, hammering out wines with amazing concentration of flavour that, thankfully, doesn't come via the expense of equally brilliant structure.

Clonakilla
Shiraz/Viognier 2003
Canberra
Australia

Shiraz – red grape blended with Viognier – white grape? Sounds bizarre but it's been happening for hundreds of years in the Côte-Rôtie region of France's Northern Rhône – and more recently in Australia.

And even though there are plenty of worthy attempts, few succeed quite like Clonakilla. This winery is a father and son operation located in Canberra (ironically HQ to both the Australian Goverment and Australia's porn industry!) and the wines, although there are few of them, rock. The wine still looks and smells like Shiraz but it has an extra dimension of aromatics (citrus and floral) courtesy of the Viognier. Check it out.

One of the things that I enjoy most about my job is the handful of surprises I get along the way. Some are nice. Some are not. Take English wine for example. On the whole, the very thought of English wine is about as attractive to me as say accidentally walking in on Josh Frost and Mr T, naked, and flapping about in an inflatable wading pool full of custard.

Trust me, this isn't a matter of sour grapes (that's actually funnier than you think!), but England just shouldn't be any good at producing wine. Football, yep. Darts, definitely. Rugby, maybe. But wine, c'mon! In fact the evidence against it is compelling. In the end, a complex equation of the wrong varieties, poor geographical location (England is about as far north of the Equator as you could ever wish to grow grapes), constant rainfall, lack of hills, not much sun, overly fertile soil, and warm beer all conspire to work against it in its bid to grow grapes.

So, all that said, you could imagine my surprise when I heard about Nyetimber – England's first bonafide wine-producing superstar (located about halfway between London and Brighton), and for obvious reasons, arguably one of the most exciting producers of sparkling wine anywhere outside of Champagne.

What makes Nyetimber – and a handful of other local producers – really special is harder to pin down, but there's no doubt that a fifteen-million-year-old vein of chalk linking Champagne and West Sussex, quite a few US dollars, and some silky French winemaking skills have all certainly helped. The result of all of this has been some stonkingly good wines, a string of great show results, and more than just the odd red-faced wine critic who has mistaken the wines for being French.

Billecart-Salmon
Brut Rosé NV
Champagne
France

get it from…

United Kingdom
£32.95

Robersons
Berry Bros & Rudd

Forget the imitators – for the better part of 200 years Billecart-Salmon have been piecing together the legendary Billecart Rosé – easily one of the world's great non vintage Champagnes.

A combination of 40% Chardonnay, 40% Pinot Noir, and 20% Pinot Meunier this wine is delicate and dry with aromas of wild strawberry, biscuit, and spice. And, while Billecart Rosé falls head first into the "bling" category, the price is far from difficult to digest.

Little short of love in a glass.

Egon Müller zu Scharzhof
Riesling 2002
Saar
Germany

get it from…

United Kingdom
£29.95

Berry Bros & Rudd

The wines that come off the
Scharzhof (black slope) are among
some of the most focused and
amazingly well-balanced wines
on the planet. Egon Müller is a man
who builds wines that run with all the
precision of a finely tuned 500SL.

Characteristically pale in colour,
these are wines which aromatically
are all about pure-citrus, slate, and
floral tones, while in the mouth they
walk that treacherous tightrope of
sweetness and acidity perfectly.

As delicate as Mum's best china,
yet built to last forever.

Mount Edward
Pinot Noir 2002
Central Otago
New Zealand

Outside of France, Pinot Noir has found few places to really call home. And while Australia and the USA continue to get their heads around this variety, New Zealand has been off and running for some time.

One of the hotspots is Central Otago (think southern end of the south island) where big investment and some very tidy wines have raised more than just a few eyebrows.

This wine has it all – beautiful aromatics that point to a tightly wound core of plum and dark-forest fruit with hints of earth and spice, not to mention some deftly handled cedary oak lurking in the shadows. The palate is generous, silky and long, and in a couple of words – absolutely rocking!

Cullen
Cabernet Sauvignon/Merlot 2000
Western Australia
Australia

get it from…

United Kingdom
£30.50

Philglas & Swiggot
Liberty Wines

Cullen Cabernet/Merlot is without doubt one of Australia's greatest wines. Margaret River superstar Vanya Cullen, runs an incredibly tight ship and is meticulous about the way she produces this big, rich Biodynamic blend of 75% Cabernet Sauvignon and 25% Merlot.

There are some pretty big raps on this wine too, with many critics believing that this Cullen wine will go down as one of the greats.

The nose is jam-packed with tightly wound cassis and dark-berried fruit right next to aromas of tobacco leaf, cedar, and sweet spice.

An absolute cracker and the perfect addition to any wine-lover's Christmas stocking!

Kiwifruits of Labour
August 13 2004, 3.36pm

At this year's Olympics, NZ took home a grand total of five medals (incidentally the same number of times Jamie used the word "f…" in episode four of Jamie's Kitchen!). Three of them were gold, the rest were silver. Not a bad result considering that Team NZ left Sydney four years ago with just three bronze medals – and even they were won with the help of a horse! Sorry Rodney.

But just imagine if winemaking was an Olympic sport – the "only" Olympic sport in fact! I reckon that 37th placed New Zealand would more than likely find themselves well up the sharp end of the leader board – the envy of the USA and maybe even on top of Australia once it was all said and done!

We all know how good Marlborough Sauvignon Blanc can be, and as a country nobody has championed the pros of the screwcap quite like the Kiwis. But where New Zealand competes comfortably on the world stage is in the production of other varieties such as Pinot Noir, Syrah, and Riesling. The best offerings of Pinot – and I'm talking about the really amazing stuff here – rank as some of the best examples to be found anywhere outside of Burgundy, while good Syrah and Riesling often point more than just the odd suggestive finger towards France and Germany respectively.

But all of this comes at a price, and a complex web of expensive varieties, microscopic productions, and a few unkind blows from Mother Nature has raised more than a couple of concerns about the viability and sustainability of a number of top-end producers and regions alike. Time will tell and watch this space…

Fontodi
Vigna del Sorbo
Chianti Classico 2001
Tuscany
Italy

get it from…

United Kingdom
£25.99

Philglas & Swiggot

They say it's the little things, the super-fine attention to detail, that gives you a competitive edge in business. When it comes to attention to detail in the world of wine, Giovanni Manetti is your man.

His Tuscan estate, Fontodi, is amongst the finest in Italy, and it's Manetti's efforts in the vineyard that put him head and shoulders above the rest. Vigna del Sorbo is a reserve version (drawing on the estate's best parcels of fruit) of the standard Fontodi Chianti Classico. Think dark Morello cherry, leather, aniseed, tobacco, and super well-integrated cedary oak. There's plenty of lush fruit in the mouth that's balanced out by trademark, dry, grippy Sangiovese tannins.

Isole e Olena
Cabernet Sauvignon 1999
Tuscany
Italy

As one of my favourite producers on the planet, the thing that I love about Isole e Olena is that while it stays true to the very traditional style of Sangiovese that it delivers year in year out it's Paulo di Marchi's work with more international varieties such as Chardonnay, Syrah, and in this case Cabernet Sauvignon that illustrates the true scale of his talents.

Concentrated and dense the nose is loaded with aromas of dark plum, cassis, and liquorice. The palate is weighty and focussed with loads of pure fruit and has brilliant structure.

This is a monster you could put in the cellar and forget about for the next ten to fifteen years. One of the best Cabernets I have ever tasted.

Joseph
Sparkling Red NV
South Australia
Australia

I'm not sure why, but fizzy red at Christmas time is a very Aussie tradition and my fave is Joseph Sparkling Red, made by Joe Grilli of Primo Estate in South Australia's Adelaide Plains. In order to understand what a labour of love the production of this wine truly is, picture this.

First of all Grilli takes multiple vintages of his own finished Amarone-style Cabernets and then blends them with a whole stack of odds and ends that he has kicking around. This gnarly concoction is then tank fermented to give it fizz, and the result just has to be tasted to believed. The current vintage is right up to scratch and just for the record, it's what I'll be drinking this coming December 25!

get it from…

United Kingdom
£22.75

Philglass & Swiggot
Bibendum

Knoll Reid
Loibenberg Riesling 2001
Wachau
Austria

Austria is hot right now, and this wine – sporting one of the most OTT labels on the planet – has to go down as one of the greatest examples of Riesling that I've ever put in my mouth. It simply blew my mind.

The show opens with aromas of fresh flowers, citrus, and exotic Asian spices and concludes with a mouthful of wine that is as precise, delicate, focused, and intense as you could ever wish. Phew!

If you have to sell vital organs to get your hands on some of this wine, then do it!

Spanish Acquisition
July 9 2004, 12.09pm

Glastonbury's just turned thirty-four and organizers officially hailed this year's event as a raging success. Best Glastonbury ever in fact! Crowds were cool, facilities fine, and most importantly, the performers shone like never before. It even rained, but that's all just part of what makes it Glastonbury.

So, what's this got to do with wine? Nothing really, but I'm just back from a tasting of over sixty wines from one of Spain's most feverishly talked about wine regions, Ribera del Duero and while searching for this weeks *Juice* inspiration, I couldn't help but draw more than just a few comparisons between Ribera del Duero and Glastonbury…

As Spain's fastest growing region, Ribera del Duero was little more than a truck stop thirty-four years ago. So expensive now is land in Ribera that John Radford, author of *The New Spain* (Mitchell Beazley *a.k.a* world's best wine publishers – x) reckons that nowadays you just about need "gold rocks" to get anywhere near it. There are lots of shiny black Range Rovers in Ribera now. It gets really cold in Ribera at night… I'm struggling aren't I?

But the most important comparison between Ribera del Duero and Glastonbury lies in the overall high-quality of the producers/performers on offer. The sixty-odd wines (all red) that I tasted were from the mind-blowingly good and sun-drenched 2001 vintage. And, even though trying to spot a regional style proved about as frustrating as trying to buy a Glastonbury ticket, all the wines were bursting at the seams with fruit and many of them ready to drink right now. The down side – and I'm sorry to say this but it's a big down side – is that fewer than twenty per cent of the wines I tasted are actually available in the UK…

Krug
Grande Cuvée NV
Champagne
France

get it from…

United Kingdom
£99.99

Oddbins

How's this for bling? One of my most memorable food and wine experiences happened about ten years ago. A couple of guys I worked with at a wine shop in Melbourne organized a private dinner party with Aussie chef Greg Brown in charge of the food. Wine aside, the highlight of the evening was witnessing Brown whisk an entire bottle of Krug Grande Cuvée through a lobster bisque to create "Krug Soup"… It was awesome.

Krug is a family owned Champagne house in Reims, France and was the original producer of super-premium Champagne. Its style is rich, yeasty, and full (thanks to a bit of time spent in wood) and the wines develop a beautiful honeyed toast character given time.

Louis Roederer
Brut Premier NV
Champagne
France

get it from…
United Kingdom
£29.99

Majestic

Images of Louis Roederer Cristal have become synonymous with bling right around the planet. Rappers have ditched "40's" in favour of it, while Formula One drivers guzzle Cristal down like water. For the rest of us there's a considerably cheaper alternative, Louis Roederer Brut Premier NV.

Brut Premier is without doubt one of the best non vintage Champagnes on the market. A 50/50 blend of Chardonnay and Pinot Noir, Brut Premier's appeal lies in the fact that it straddles the fence being a nice compromise somewhere between the leaner aperitif styles of fizz and the often top-heavy food styles.

Go tell that to your posse!

Mas de Daumas
Gassac 2002
Languedoc
France

I first read about Mas de Daumas Gassac in Kermit Lynch's classic *Adventures on the Wine Route* (a killer book if you can find a copy). Since then I've had the pleasure of trying a few bottles! Relying heavily on Cabernet as the base of this multi-tiered blend, MdDG couldn't look anymore un-Cabernet like if it tried!

The wine is deeply fruited and spicy – more like you might expect from Syrah found in the not too distant Rhône Valley. Flavour-wise the wine is a full-bodied mouthful of plum, cassis, and minerals. Many examples live to a ripe old age. Find a good retailer, get them to order you some if they don't already carry it, and then stash them away for special occasions only!

Michelot Meursault
2001
Burgundy
France

get it from…

United Kingdom
£19.95

Berry Bros & Rudd

If you're one of those people who fall into the "don't like Chardonnay" camp, then this wine is your baby! Meursault is a French village in the Côte d'Or widely regarded for its fatter, fuller style of Chardonnay, and Michelot are certainly doing their job of keeping up local appearances!

This wine is an exercise in proving that Chardonnay can be both big and beautiful. Stuffed full of ripe grapefruit, grilled hazelnuts, and burnt toffee and spice, Michelot Meursault represents insanely good wine for the outlay. Get on board.

Pesquera
2002
Ribero del Duero
Spain

Officially sporting one of the world's coolest wine labels (check out the bling gold trim!), Pesquera is the big brother of Condado de Haza, and the brainchild of the legendary Alexandro Fernandez – arguably one of Ribera del Duero's finest and most important producers

Pesquera is carved from 100% Tinto Fino (Tempranillo) and – thanks to some fancy footwork in the winery – comes packing some serious dark plummy fruit and well-handled spicy oak.

Nothing short of magic.

Penfolds
RWT Shiraz 2000
South Australia
Australia

Playing second fiddle to big brother Grange in the Penfolds camp, RWT (Red Wine Trial) is made from select parcels of old-vine Shiraz from a mix of South Australia's finest grape-growing areas, and then fermented in new French oak (Grange sees American oak). It is rivalled only by its older sibling and, like Grange, RWT is never entered into shows.

Intense purple in colour, the wine oozes aromas of blood plum, cassis, liquorice, cedar, and freshly ground pepper. The palate is rich and seamless with weight and intensity. The power of the fruit is matched wickedly by soft acidity and firm drying tannin. Beautifully balanced, and built for the long haul. Stick it away or decant it and enjoy with good friends.

Planet Organic
July 23 2004, 12.31pm

"Why don't you write something about organic wine this week?" suggested Carls, as we waited in line at the local health food shop. "Maybe," I replied. Maybe not.

Call me old fashioned, but whenever I come across a wine label with the word organic printed in fluorescent pink, large type type, and bold font, alarm bells can't help but ring out. But then again, that was twice in one week. Maybe this was a sign. Just days earlier Fifteen had been reviewed, and the question asked "How many organic wines do you have on your list?" More alarm bells. Organic wines on the list… I'm not sure? Quite a few I reckon. I've since found out that I have none.

Organic wine is defined as "any wine made from organically grown grapes" – and this is the really important bit – "without the addition of sulphites". And without banging on too much, sulphites are preservatives that stop your wine turning brown and tasting rubbish. Pretty important inclusion I'd have thought? Not as far as organics are concerned. You see sulphites are also classed as a synthetic additive, and that is definitely not organic.

What I do have a lot of on my list are wines that have been made from organically grown grapes. These are grapes grown without the use of industrial fertilisers, herbicides, fungicides, and pesticides. Wines that are treated organically right up to the point where the winemaker – thankfully – throws in a good-old dose of sulphur dioxide.

The other major benefit of being organic only up to a point is that it gives grape-growers and winemakers alike, the flexibility to intervene should they need to. Better still they don't even have to make mention of it on the label!

Crokov Estate
The Dominator 2001
Ferjudsa
Crokovia

I don't have to tell you all about how big Merlonay's going to be – you know. That said you should definitely take a look at this variety's greatest offering to date. Set to join the company of iconic wines like Grange, "The Dominator" is serious special occasion – just married, new baby, recently divorced, successful sex change, new job, just fired – kind of stuff.

Having spent a whopping sixty months in brand-new Crokovian oak, and displaying a seriously flashy, three-quarter palate, this wine is all class.

Tread carefully though or the lazy 16.5 degrees of alcohol will have your head spinning harder than a Tony Hawk 900.

Torres
Mas La Plana 1999
Penedès
Spain

get it from…

United Kingdom
£20.99

Sainsbury's

PRODUCER OF THE YEAR

Hammered together by Torres, Mas la Plana is Spain's finest example of Cabernet Sauvignon. Even more impressive is that this single-vineyard Cabernet took first place at the uber-exclusive 1970 Paris Wine Olympiad beating some of the biggest (mainly French!) wine names on the planet for first place. No mean feat.

I love this wine because it has heaps going on apart from just fruit. There are incredible aromas of earth, undergrowth, cedar, smoke, and spice all wrapped around a solid core of dark plum and cassis. Go treat yourself.

Index

A
A-Mano 123
Allegrini 133
Almaviva 152
Alvaro Palacios 153
Amyethystos 69
Annie's Lane 37
Ata Rangi 156
Au Bon Climat 157

B
Banrock Station 108
Barbera 17
Barolo 151
Basa 10, 46
Baume, La 31
Biblia Chora 91
Big House Red 82
Billecart-Salmon 164
Bonny Doon 82
Bowen Estate 113
Brown Bros. 34, 40

C
Cabernet Sauvignon 17
Campbells of Rutherglen 98
Cape Mentelle 105
Carmènere 18
Casal di Serra, 35
Casillero del Diablo 27
Catena 54, 114

Cerro del Masso 52
Chardonnay 11
Château de Beaucastel 158
Châteauneuf-du-Pape 117, 158
Chivite Gran Feudo 36
Clonakilla 161
Crokov Estate 188
Cullen 169

D
d'Arenberg 136
Dehesa Gago, 119
Delta Vineyard 12
The Dominator 188
Dr Loosen 29

E
Egon Müller zu Schwarhof 165
Escudo 137

F
Fairview 45
Falesco 96
Fontodi 172
Frescobaldi 147

G
Gaia 146
Gamekeeper's Red 49
Garganega 11
Geoff Merrill 41

Gewurtztraminer 12
Giesen 76
Goats do Roam 45
Green Point 93
Grenache 18
Grover Vineyards 125
Grüner Veltiner 12
Guigal 68
La Guita 30

H
Hewitson 116
Hugel 127
Huia 144

I
Isole e Olena 173

J
Jermann 142
Joseph 174

K
Knappstein 85
Knoll Reid 175
Kooyung 101
Kostas Lazaridis 69
Krug 178

L
Labirinto, Il 112
Lindemans 44
Louis Roederer 179

M
Majella 150
Malbec 18
Marsanne 12
Mas de Daumas Gassac 180
Mas la Plana 189
Merlonay 86
Merlot 18, 38
Metala 83
Michelot Meursault 182
Montana 61
Mount Edward 166
Mourvèdre 18-19
MR Moscatel 131
Mudhouse 84
Muscat 12-13

N
Naked Grape, The 58
Nebbiolo 19
Negroamaro 19
Notios, 146

O
Orange Muscat & Flora 40

P
Palliser 90
Pedro Ximenez 13, 100
Penfolds 184

Perrin et Fils 117
Pesquera 183
Petit Chablis 109
Pieropan 122
Pinot Blanc 13
Pinot Gris 13
Pinot Meunier 19
Pinot Noir 19-20, 120
Planeta 97
Poderi Aldo Conterno 151
Poggerino 112
Porcupine Ridge 60
Prager 160
Primitivo 20
Primus, 75

Q
Quatroventi 132

R
Ravenswood 42
Rèmole, 147
Riesling 13-16, 64
Roussanne 16
RTW, 184

S
St Hallet 49
Sangiovese 20
Sangre de Toro, 33

Sauvignon Blanc 16
Segreta, La 97
Sémillon 16
Shaw and Smith 103
Stella Bella 74
Stonecroft 88
Syrah 20-1

T
Tamar Ridge 130
Tatachilla 48
Terrasses, Les 153
Terruzzi & Puthod 143
Torres 9, 26, 33, 55, 189
Trimbach 104

U
Umani Ronchi Verdicchio 25

V
Valdespino 100
Vasse Felix 78
Veramonte Primus 75
Verdicchio 17
Vernaccia di San Gimignano 143
Viña Esmeralda 26
Viña Rodríguez 10, 46, 119, 131

Vigna del Sorbo 172
Vitiano 96
Viognier 17

W
William Fèvre 109
Wirra Wirra 71

Y
Yalumba 63, 92
Yarra Bank 138

Z
ZD, Green Point 93
Zonte's Footstep 8, 79

Mitchell Beazley would like to thank the following for their help in sourcing bottle images:
Adnams, John Armit, Australian Wine Services, Beringer Blass, Berkmann, Bibendum, Brown Brothers UK, Les Caves de Pyrenne Ltd, Charles Hawkins, Concha y Toro UK, Constellation, Dean Hewitson, Dreyfuss Ashby, Eclectic Wines, Enotria, Fairview, Farr Vintners, Heyman Barwell Jones Ltd, HWCG, JE Fells, Lea & Sandeman, Liberty Wines, Lindsey May PR, Lion Nathan UK, Maison Marques et Domaines, Majella, Moët Hennessey, Negotiants UK, Novum, Oddbins, Paragon, Siegel Wine Agencies, Stella Bella, Lucy Bridgers and Torres, Western Wines.

Cheers

This guide is dedicated to all the amazing people I have the privilege of working with day in day out; Fifteen Restaurant, Fifteen Foundation, Fresh Partners, Sweet as Candy, Fresh One, The Plant, The Flour Station, Fresh Spaces – you guys were originally, are now, and will continue to be, the inspiration for writing *The Juice*. Thank you x

Also, a big fat juicy thank you going out to the following.

Carls for never-ending love and support, and endless good *Juice* ideas! Thanks baby x

Matt Utber and The Plant for dressing it up nicely – your Midas touch in the design department has brought this project to life.

Chris Terry who saddled up once again for *The Juice* – not bad for a cartographer! As ever, thanks for everything mate.

The incredible duo of "mums-to-be" Hilary Lumsden and Yasia Williams-Leedham (we made it and thank you! x), Jane, Tim, Fi, Sarah, Kate, Mark, Martin, and the rest of the gang at Mitchell Beazley. Sandy and all the crew at Hardie Grant Australia.

My right hand man, Paul Green, as usual thanks for everything.

Jamie for the golden moments in front of my mum! Lisa Sullivan and Sally Gregory at Fresh Partners. Jeni Barnett and Prospect Pictures (*Great Food Live* and *Saturday Kitchen*). Danny for all number of things, and Kelly Cooper for the legs!

Mum, Drew, Caroline, Anne, Thommo, Gin, Camilla, Tobe, Randy, Gyros, BP and CC, Philip, The Jones and Duncan clans, Victoria Bitter, The Hawks, and beautiful Melbourne town – love and miss you all.

Happy Drinking Always

M x